THE COMPLETE

QUINCY JONES

THE COMPLETE

QUINCY JONES

MY JOURNEY & PASSIONS

by QUINCY JONES

Preface
MAYA ANGELOU

Foreword
CLINT EASTWOOD

Introduction
BONO

Afterword
SIDNEY POITIER

INSIGHT EDITIONS

San Rafael, California

title page: Phil Woods, Q, Oliver Nelson, Wayne Andre
with the Quincy Jones Band.

opposite: Holding a gift from Dizzy Gillespie of his
original engraved Martin trumpet. Engraved on the bell is
a treble clef with the melody to "Ooh Bop She Bam" and,
above, "Diz."

INSIGHT 👁 EDITIONS

17 Paul Drive : San Rafael : CA : 94903
phone 415.526.1370 • fax 415.526.1394
www.insighteditions.com

Library of Congress Cataloging-in-Publication Data available.

ISBN-13: 978-1-933784-67-0

10 9 8 7 6 5 4 3 2 1

ROOTS of PEACE   ✸ REPLANTED PAPER

Palace Press International, in association with Roots of Peace, will plant
two trees for each tree used in the manufacturing of this book. Roots
of Peace is an internationally renowned humanitarian organization
dedicated to eradicating land mines worldwide and converting war-torn
lands into productive farms and wildlife habitats. Together, we will
plant two million fruit and nut trees in Afghanistan and provide farmers
there with the skills and support necessary for sustainable land use.

Printed in China by
Palace Press International
www.palacepress.com

During the *Free and Easy* musical in 1959 in Paris at Alhambra Theatre.

CONTENTS

PREFACE
Maya Angelou
IX

FOREWORD
Clint Eastwood
XI

INTRODUCTION
Bono
XIII

1: THE EARLY DAYS
1

4: MENTORING A BETTER WORLD
74

2: THE MUSIC BUSINESS
22

5: LIFE & LEGACY
104

3: FILM & TELEVISION
52

ACKNOWLEDGEMENTS
140

AFTERWORD
Sidney Poitier
138

Preface
MAYA ANGELOU

I LIKE MANY WOMEN, and I suspect even a few men, I have always been a little in love with Quincy Jones. I have taken him as a brother friend because he reminds me a lot of my only sibling. Bailey Johnson, my brother, was the closest my family came to making a genius. He was two years older than I, and at full growth was five feet, five inches tall, and I measured six feet by the time I had reached fifteen. Bailey explained to me that since I was female, I should expect kind treatment from men. They should open doors for me and hold my chair when I sat at a table. They should have good senses of humor and be good at anything they do.

Quincy was breathtakingly handsome and had a good sense of humor. He held my chair when I went to sit down, he was considerably shorter than I, and he liked me. Obviously he had all of the necessary qualities to make him a good brother.

I first met Quincy in the Sixties when a friend at UCLA had arranged for writers and musicians to give lectures at the university. Quincy was scoring the music for the movie *For Love of Ivy*, which starred Sidney Poitier, Carroll O'Connor, and Abbey Lincoln. He asked if I would write the lyrics for two songs to be sung by blues legend B. B. King. We worked together and laughed together, and one of our two songs, "You Put It on Me," reached the top ten.

Because his interests ranged far and wide, I asked him how he could include all genres of music. He said when he and Ray Charles were young, Ray was the band leader, and he once informed his musicians that he had signed them to play for a Polish wedding. Quincy said he told Ray, "Man, I'm a jazz musician; I don't play polka." Whereupon Ray turned to him and said, "Good music is good music, man, don't be a fool all your life."

Quincy Delight Jones, Jr., is more than an American treasure. He is the entire treasure chest. I, too, have continued to work in the United States, Europe, and Africa, and I notice the further our ambitions take us, the closer we are. I value the man, his music, and his serious and sunny self.

You go on, Quincy, you boy. I will have "lurnch" with you anytime you say!

L to R: Maya Angelou, Oprah Winfrey, Q, Jolie Jones at Maya's 80th birthday party, hosted by Oprah in West Palm Beach.

opposite: Rehearsing while stranded with his big band in New York. Person on left is Elijah Hodges.

Foreword
CLINT EASTWOOD

BACK WHEN I WAS a teenager, I used to go down to Seattle University to hear a big swing band they had. They were pretty darn good for a college band, and this young fellow called Quincy was not only the trumpet player but sort of the charismatic character of the band—a great-looking guy, a chick magnet. Everyone liked Quincy, and he was the kind who just liked everybody. He never seemed to hold any animosity towards people with other ideas or of different nationalities, a very open-borders kind of man, something you can also tell just from listening to his music. For a guy who loves jazz and other forms of really fine music, he's done stuff in genres that you wouldn't expect him to do. He's not afraid to step out and do things that are outside his vernacular, his upbringing.

Later we became acquainted in Hollywood, when I was working at Universal. All of a sudden people were starting to reach out and go towards more modern big band music for movie scores, and he was right in the forefront of that, one of the pioneers of using jazz in films. But he was also busy doing a lot of projects, one after the other, so we never could get him for ours. He was the sort of guy who took advantage of every opportunity to go on to the next stage of his life, and he'll do that until he drops. I admire that.

Up until the time he had his aneurysms in the mid-1970s, he played the trumpet very, very well. After that, of course, he could never play again, which, on one hand, is a terrible shame. But on the other hand, he has contributed a tremendous amount to the music industry by being forced to be more than just a performer. To have bounced back from all that—something beyond mere human tenacity helped out there.

Having now been a great friend of Quincy's for many years, I've been able to fully appreciate how his qualities as a man and mentor go way beyond the purely musical, also enriching the lives of so many others on a deeply personal level. Quincy loves to pontificate and relate little anecdotal stories about music and life, as you'll see in the book you're about to read. But they're always appealing because they speak to everyone, not just to people who know music from the inside.

Quincy's interested in what he's doing, but he's also interested in what *other* people are doing, and that's what makes him great. My son is a musician, and Quincy always asks about him. Quincy's always got a lot of things going, and that's what keeps him young, and keeps his mind clicking on all eight. He also is deeply concerned with people who have less opportunity than he has had along the way, reaching out to the kids all over the world and getting them on track to being involved in something besides just hanging out. He loves to see young kids in rural or destitute areas get a chance to express themselves. There's a generosity that's just built into him.

He's amazing the way he utilizes his time; it's very hard to keep up with him. I can only concentrate on one project at a time, and I have to stay with it. It seems like Quincy can do at least two or three things at once. Let's say he's off in Europe or Africa or Russia on some project. Then he'll call me up and say he's just re-recorded *The Good, The Bad and The Ugly* with Herbie Hancock. And he says, 'You've got to hear it,' so I'll go over to his house, and he'll play it and say, 'Listen to this part; listen to that part.' Every time I see him, we also get to have a lot of laughs.

If I had to sum up what Quincy Jones has given the world, I would tell people to look at his versatility and at all the things he's done for others, whether it's philanthropic or within his profession. He shows us you may have adversity come along in life, but you can overcome and expand beyond it. He typifies that, and he has helped a whole lot of people get off onto a good track. He'll keep on doing that for a good long while because just when you think he's going to lay quiet, he comes up with something else and is cruising right along. I guarantee if I call him this afternoon, there's going to be at least one whole new deal he's working on. The legacy he'll leave to the world is genuinely tremendous.

At Bono's castle in Dublin.

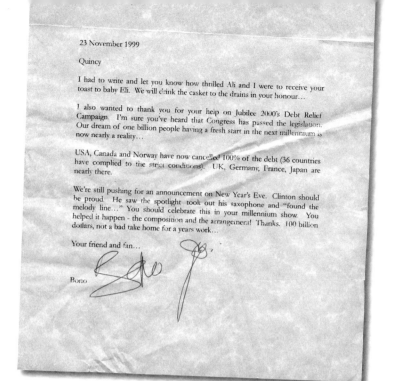

Introduction
BONO

QUINCY JONES WAS TOO COOL for cool … so he reinvented the whole concept … made aloof engaged, made elitist get off the bus and press the flesh … His rebirth of the cool involved intense heat, his cool would be hot like a Brazilian beauty, hot like an African queen, hot like the sticky streets of New York in the summer, the sweat of the rhythms he would bring to popular music … The intense warmth of the man himself offered a new kind of sexiness to the way a music mogul could carry himself.

I have a picture in my head—I think it was taken by the great Herman Leonard—of Q in the studio with Miles Davis in the late '50s, conducting the room (and himself) in a silent and elegant way that just makes all the huffing and puffing, pushing and pulling of musical ambition look so … eh … un-cool.

That must be why I first attempted to glue myself to the man.

Irish people were not brought into the world to be cool … noisy, funny, literate, maybe … musical, verbose, feisty, fighty, maybe … but not cool.

This is lucky for me … 'cos I couldn't have been there if I tried. Even Frank Sinatra, when he first saw us, told a Las Vegas audience, "Wow … these Irish guys are number one, but they haven't spent a dime on their clothes."

I went to study the new cool at Quincy's house in Los Angeles about twenty years ago to the day as I write this. Myself and Ali were late, on our way home from somewhere, and talking about my wife's still favorite subject: who was I going to be when I grew up? I offered the name Quincy Jones as a person I had always admired but could never hope to be, the man who has, more than any other, made music uniquely relevant to five decades. In what felt like an instant, Charlie, who was driving us, without saying a word, pulled up outside Quincy's house. He'd called and had gotten us invited over. It was two a.m., and we still remember the shock of entering Q's late-night world in every detail.

There was the man himself, elegant as always, soft spoken and a little more interested in the company of women than men, making Ali feel at home in his home and pointing out to the rock star a large bronze sculpture, of an exaggerated figure of a black man sticking his neck out, in the hall.

"It's called attitude."

"What? Owning a piece like that?" I inquired.

"No, the piece is called *Attitude*."

Q doesn't know how to not be himself, and he makes everyone around him want to be themselves. In fact, it's when you are not yourself with him, that's when you get in trouble. Everyone was welcome in this place, as long as they brought their actual selves with them … My guess was that a new idea was the price of admission, that and old-school loyalty. Lionel Richie was there that night, another scholar from the school of the true gentleman. Quincy, it appeared, went fishing at night for friends, for fun, for ideas, for music. He would hang his hat anywhere there was a hook, but over the years there were more hooks in Q's house than anywhere else.

"Everybody's welcome" meant every genre was welcome. It's why he could work with Peggy Lee one day

This innovator who hung with the Count and the Duke, who was on the board with the Chairman, the consigliere to the kings and queens of pop, the envy of Prince and the Boss, is, as it turns out, as humble as a peasant and as confident as the President, which, I realize, he is. ~ BONO

and Chaka Khan the next. As a record producer, Q does not try to turn singers into vehicles for his voice. He brings out *their* voice.

On that night in 1988, Quincy told me about getting a call from Sinatra about going back into the studio to start a new album. The Chairman had simply said, "Q, it's time to shake up the citizens." "Shaking up the citizens starts at home, doesn't it?" Quincy said. "We got to challenge ourselves, though."

We left as an orange sun lit his trees and began to fill his glass house. He kissed us goodbye.

"It's great to be alive." I said.

"Great to be alive?" he said, "GREAT TO BE ALIVE?? … IT'S CRUCIAL, MAN."

Think forward a hundred years or so. In 2108, most music fans may not be certain of the sequence of music from the twentieth century. Did Elvis Presley come before or after hip-hop? Was Louis Armstrong around at the same time as Eminem? Chronology gets fuzzy with distance. In the future, all music will be set on permanent shuffle.

But music lovers who are not yet born will remember the records that Quincy Jones produced, arranged, wrote, and/or played on. They will know Ray Charles, they will know *Thriller*, Lena Horne, Sarah Vaughan, *Sanford and Son*, Count Basie, *Roots*, Norah Jones, *Body Heat*, Duke Ellington, *In the Heat of the Night*, Dizzy Gillespie,

Frank Sinatra, Miles Davis, "We Are the World," and "It's My Party."

The wonder will be that one man could have fit so much music into one lifetime. Q had better get his evidence in order now, or in centuries to come historians will wonder if there were two, three, four of him. Archaeologists will be excavating for a Q cloning factory; scientists will be trying to identify a Q gene. He will be known as a musical Shakespeare: could one person really have done all that?

But we know. Quincy not only did all that, he did all that while scoring for Steven Spielberg and Bill Cosby, while doing charity work from America to Africa, while raising seven remarkable children, and while always having a good time.

Q is the sort of man you want to have with you whether you're going to church or robbing a bank. He appreciates the high life and a bit of the low life, as I say. He doesn't care where you are from; it's your story he's interested in. His story told here is an extraordinary one. A musical genius, an effortless showman, an old-fashioned gentleman, whose brain is as big as his heart and nearly as big as his libido. It's rare in this world to meet someone who is equally relaxed on the stage in Vegas, in a back alley in Accra, at Carnaval in Bahia—where we were nearly trampled to death—or in the grandeur of the Vatican.

I can personally testify to this; I am a witness. In 1999, Quincy and I traveled to meet Pope John Paul II together. We were involved with the Jubilee 2000 Drop the Debt Campaign, a worldwide attempt to get governments to cancel the old, unpayable debts of the poorest countries. We headed for the outskirts of Rome on a mission to enlist the Pope's support. I cannot speak for Quincy, but I confess I was a little intimidated as we entered Castle Gandofo, impressed by the sense of mystery and authority, by the Swiss Guard with their muskets and their uniforms designed by Leonardo Da Vinci. The Pontiff was very frail. I was moved by the heroic effort he made just to stand and greet each one of us. Amid all the grandeur and trepidation, Quincy whispered to me, "Check … out … the shoes." The shoes of the fisherman on this particular day were burgundy wingtips with light tan ribbed socks. Q said softly with admiration in his voice, "The cat is wearing some pimp shoes. Stylin'!"

Quincy does not distinguish high and low. Only good and bad. "We Are the World" is not only the title of his greatest hit—it's how he looks at life. As a musician, what an honor it is to have lived in Quincy Jones' century; as a person, what a privilege to call him a friend. No matter what shoes you wear.

If God has a jukebox, I know which name is on more of the selections than any other. It starts with Q. It ends there, too.

Bono and Q discussing the pimp shoes.

opposite: At a dinner celebrating Bono's Martin Luther King award.

1

THE EARLY
YEARS

It seems like only yesterday that I was 13 years old in Seattle,
passionately awaiting the big bands that came to town.
I stood paralyzed by the aura of these talented, dignified,
fun, totally original, global-minded masters. ~ Q

THE EARLY YEARS

QUINCY JONES IS the most successful Renaissance man in the history of American popular music. That's quite a boast, and not one that the modest man is likely to claim for himself should you get him in a corner. But look at the facts. Can he produce? Only the biggest selling album of all time, Michael Jackson's *Thriller*, not to mention the chart-busting single that got forty-six mega-stars in the same room at the same time, "We Are the World." Can he do anything else? Only compose, arrange, orchestrate, and play any brass instrument you can think of. Can he hang onstage and in the studio with the best of them? Louis Armstrong, Dizzy Gillespie, Count Basie, Duke Ellington, Ray Charles, Frank Sinatra, Peggy Lee, Aretha Franklin, Paul Simon, Michael Jackson, George Benson, Donna Summer, Gloria Estefan, Celine Dion, Bono, Ice T—those are just a few of the legends he's worked intimately with over the last several decades.

You'd think that's enough to not only keep a man busy, but keep him from even finding enough time to sleep. But Quincy's never one to let the grass grow under his feet, at the age of twenty-five or seventy-five, eventually becoming a universally respected figure, whose reach extends to all walks of life. He's also somehow managed to find time to make hit solo records under his own name, and score dozens of hit movies and television shows. And he's not content to do nothing but music, either, also producing hit movies, TV shows, and world-uniting concerts; creating the foremost hip-hop magazine, *Vibe*; and entrepreneurial achievements such as owning and operating TV and radio stations, in addition to several major international humanitarian programs.

If you've been alive at any time since 1950, you've also heard, seen, or been affected by something Quincy had a big-time hand in—and you'll probably continue to do so for the rest of your life. So, in fact, will your parents and kids. What's most amazing is that

previous page: Bumps Blackwell Band at the Washington Educational and Social Club, Seattle, c. 1949.

opposite: Q and Major Pigford, aka the Benzadreen and Methadreen comedy team.

They pinned my hand to a wooden fence with a switchblade when I was seven years old. ~ Q

Q's father's original saw from 1928, which he used until the 1960s, and his union cards from 1949.

Quincy's work reaches across all generations and styles, from jazz and pop to funk, R&B, and rap. Throughout his seventy-five years, however, Quincy has never lost sight of his deep roots in big band and jazz, and of making sure to pay serious "props" (kudos) to the many mentors who inspired him to develop his core skills.

When he was born Quincy Delight Jones, Jr., in Chicago on March 14, 1933, odds were against his even making it out of the poverty suffered by so many blacks in the Depression era, let alone becoming one of Hollywood's prime movers and shakers. His highly educated mother suffered from a mental illness that eventually led to institutionalization. His carpenter father had trouble finding work at a time when discrimination against blacks was rampant and ended up using his saw in the service of some of the biggest and baddest gangsters in Chicago, such as the original Triple O-Gs.

"All I ever saw when I was a kid were stogies, back rooms of liquor stores with two-way mirrors, guys with machine guns, and tables with piles of money on them," Quincy remembers today. "We saw this every day—people blown away, guys hanging on telephone poles with ice picks in their necks. They pinned my hand to a wooden fence with a switchblade when I was seven years old. My daddy hit one of them in the head with a hammer; one of them stuck an ice pick in my temple. That was everyday life in Chicago! Your biggest challenge every day was getting to school and getting home alive."

But Quincy would make it out of his Chicago ghetto by the age of ten, moving with his father and brother Lloyd to the Bremerton shipyards near Seattle. Then as now, a life of crime was a big temptation for young blacks like Quincy. When there's not much in the way of parental or community guidance, or even role models of your race making it big in respectable professions, it's hard to stay off the street and out of trouble. "There's nobody to tell you what to do to get you out of this," he explains. "My dad was busy all the time; he had eight kids, and was making $55 a week."

Fortunately for both Jones and the millions of listeners who'd groove to his music over the next few decades, Quincy *did* find a more creative outlet for his talents. It not only kept him out of serious trouble; it became his new community, a universal one not chained

The annotations on the photos read: Freddey Smed, Waymond Miller "Pirimp" Jones, Eddie Beard, Oscar Holden "Shift" Tatum, GRACE HOLDEN, Young Bops

to any home or city. "I was still just singing and playing piano and alto sax, when the big bands started coming through," is how he sets the scene. "Count Basie, Woody Herman, the Duke [Ellington]—I'd be at every one. And I said, '*This* is where I want to live for the rest of my life. And I want to be an arranger and a composer.'"

Jones was already something of a boy prodigy on a closetful of numerous instruments by the time he reached his teens, which would come in handy later, as he has the rare talent to score big-band music by composing personalized music for every single instrument in it.

He also knew that to become a pro and get on the bandstand, he'd have to not just play like an adult but *act* like one. Already he was brazen enough to seek tips and encouragement from as many older musicians as he could, whether they were in Seattle or just passing through town. "Most people don't understand; Seattle was one of the jumpin'-est, hottest towns in America during World War II," he points out. "Because that was the gateway to the Pacific theater—Iwo Jima, Japan, and all that stuff. It was on fire." One of his local role models was bandleader Bumps

Blackwell, who went on to produce Little Richard's hits. There was also a young Ray Charles, not much older than Quincy himself, but already living alone and getting by on just playing music, even as a blind teenager thousands of miles from home. It wasn't long before Quincy and Ray were playing, arranging, and writing together in jam sessions—bonding both as musicians and over the years, close, lifelong friends.

From farther afield came both musical inspiration and life lessons from Clark Terry, "who taught me how to correct my embouchure, and was also very influential on Miles Davis. Clark is still the greatest trumpet player alive. Then Count Basie kind of adopted me at thirteen. He sat me down and said, 'Youngblood, I'm going to tell you how black show business works. It's all about the hills and the valleys'—the hills being a metaphor for success. 'The valleys, that's when you find out what you're made out of. Because when it gets tough, then you find out what you really are.'"

Quincy was impatient to get out on the road and, at the age of fifteen, was asked to join jazz great Lionel Hampton's band—only to be taken off

top left and right: The Charlie Taylor Band in 1947 at the YMCA; it was Q's very first gig. Each musician received $7 apiece.

above: L to R: Charlie Taylor, Buddy Catlett, Q, and Billy Johnson on bass.

I played tuba, sousaphone, B-flat baritone horn, E-flat alto peck horn, French horn, trombones—because the trombones in the marching band were up near the baton-twirling majorettes. I had to be a little practical, you know! Finally I got back on trumpet, which was my love, and I started professionally on trumpet. ~ Q

the bus at the last minute for being too young. It was a crushing blow to come so close so soon, but it could have been a blessing in disguise. An underage kid traveling and playing with a jazz star was probably asking for trouble. More importantly, Jones could now finish his high school education and improve on what was becoming his chief instrument. After starting on piano, "I played tuba, sousaphone, B-flat baritone horn, E-flat alto peck horn, French horn, trombones—because the trombones in the marching band were up near the baton-twirling majorettes. I had to be a little practical, you know! Finally I got back on trumpet, which was my love, and I started professionally on trumpet."

Quincy moved to Boston after high school graduation to attend Schillinger House (later known as the Berklee College of Music) on scholarship, but it wouldn't be long before Lionel Hampton gave Quincy another chance

to join his band. This time, he took it—and never looked back. By the end of 1951, he'd composed and arranged Hampton's "Kingfish" single. When you needed a taste of smooth spice for your session, Quincy was your man, and he'd do the same thing for lots of other jazz and R&B discs in the '50s. And after European tours with Hampton and world tours with Dizzy Gillespie, he was ready for an even bigger gig—leading an international tour with a big band of his own.

top left: Celebrating his birthday on the road with the Lionel Hampton band.

top right: With Dinah Washington at Birdland.

center right: Q was the secretary for the Charlie Taylor Band.

right: "Kingfish," Q's first recording as composer, arranger, and trumpet soloist.

opposite: In Seattle, age 14, adopting the pose of a world-weary musician. The cigarette is a prop to get to play nightclubs—he didn't smoke.

top left: Q's mother, Sarah Francis Wells Jones.

top right: 1930s South Side of Chicago.

opposite: Quincy Delight Jones, Sr. and Jr.

GROWING UP

"MY MOTHER WAS a very brilliant lady," reminisces Quincy. "She went through Boston University in the '20s and '30s, [knew] ten or twelve languages, written and spoken. But she had dementia breakouts that probably could have probably been cured by vitamin B, but they didn't know that then, and for black ladies, nobody cared. So she was institutionalized when I was seven years old.

"My father was really my parent. Something that he told us every day, my brother and I, he said: 'Once a task has just begun, never leave it till it's done, be the labor great or small, do it well or not at all.' *Every* day he told us that. That probably saved us, too, because it gave us a sense of excellence and pride of craftsmanship."

Quincy and his brother Lloyd needed that sort of firm hand to keep from getting swallowed up by the mean streets of their tough Chicago neighborhood. Life in the Windy City ended with a jolt when the Jones Boys—not Quincy and Lloyd, but black gangsters for whom Quincy Jones, Sr., worked as a carpenter—got run out of town by Al Capone, "once they found out how much money they were making. And

Daddy comes to the barbershop to pick up my brother and I, and says, 'We're leaving.' I say, 'Can we get our toys?' He said, 'We don't have time.' We got on a Trailways bus and went all the way to the Northwest. We went to the Bremerton shipyards, and they had a place way out of town called Sinclair Heights. We had to walk up a hill forever, three miles. That's where they put all the black people."

Yet Quincy's not one to let any bitterness over his boyhood hardships linger. "There's a book called *Too Soon Old, Too Late Smart*," he stresses, "and it says something that I've believed in a long time: 'The statute of limitations has expired for all childhood traumas.' Get over it and get on with your life. Fix it and move on. Some of our most successful people have had some terrible childhoods." Such as another, only slightly older, local musician—blind from the age of six, and yet more recently arrived in Seattle from a far-flung corner of the country—named Ray Charles, with whom Quincy would form one of his first and most lasting musical alliances and personal friendships.

"When I got to Bremerton, an armory was our recreation center," recalls Quincy. "We heard there was a

So

V

ck
at
nd

id,
re
d

at
at

Photographs

Quincy Jones, Musical Prodigy, Studies at Seattle University

By LEO HANDLEY

Though he has his own band and has had his arrangements played by such name bands as Count Basie and Bumps Blackwell, Freshman Music Major Quincy Jones still elects to complete his course at S.U. before going on to further study.

Though this is his first year here, he made his debut in S.U. music circles last year when his descriptive suite, "The Four Winds," was played at the spring concert. He plays the trumpet and the piano.

The same arrangement of "The Four Winds" is scheduled to be played by Lionel Hampton at "Bop City" in New York in the near future, Quincy disclosed.

A graduate of Garfield High School, where he was active in the school band, Quincy is at S.U. on a music scholarship.

When asked his plans for the future, he replied, "I would like to study at Westlake Music College in Hollywood, and later to write serious studies for the movies — mood music, they call it."

Having had his own band for

QUINCY JONES

six months, "The Silhouettes," Quincy was on tour in Canada this summer and has since played at several high school and college fraternity affairs in Seattle.

"I appreciate the good in all classes of music, from boogie on up to the classics," he declared when questioned on his musical

preference. "However," he went on, "at present I have a leaning toward popular dance music."

Quincy disclosed also that he has on different occasions within the last two and a half years played with Bumps Blackwell, Cab Calloway, and Billy Eckstein.

Asked his opinion of S.U. and the students, he replied, "The instructors are cooperative and the students are tops. Everyone is very friendly."

'50 ARR

JAN JOHNSON—Entered from Bremerton High; Assistant Editor, Reporter, Messenger; Roll President; Sen Gift, Red Cross Committees; Gold Seal; Chorus; M Wintr Concert; Operetta; Honor Roll.

WILLIAM A. JOHNSON—Ski Club; Mid-Winter Co cert; Funfest; Operetta; Band; Orchestra; Libre Clerk.

JOHN JOLLY—Sports Editor, Arrow; Feature Editor, A row; Photo Club.

ETTA JONES—Entered from Alabama; Senior Play; M Winter Concert; Funfest; Roll Secretary; Friendsh Committee; Study Hall Clerk; Spring Play.

QUINCY JONES JR.—Operetta; Pen Staff Artist; Choru Orchestra; Band; Mid-Winter Concert; Noon Progre Committee; Student Director of Swing Band; Funfe

JEANIE JOY—Mid-Winter Concert; Operetta; Choru Usher, P.Q., Senior Prom Committees; Study Hall Cle

JIN JEE JUE—Funfest; Cathay Club; Ski Club; Art Co mittee.

HARRY KADOSHIMA—Secretary, Junior Class; G Seal; Honor Roll; Roll Secretary; Roll Vice-Preside Honor Society Representative; Intramural Sports; Fu fest.

YONE KANDA—Head Typist, Pen; Honor Society Rep sentative; Gold Seal; Funfest; Historian, "G" Cl Honor Roll; President, "G" Club; Ticket Committ Gym Office Clerk; "G" Club, After-School Sports.

At a Glance

from behind one of the clouds, came the moon, like a rn pushing through the haze.
JOYCE MURRAY, JUNIOR

But as a composer dreams on and on
And his dreams are hopeless, it seems,
Even if people don't listen,
He can always thank God for his dreams.
QUINCY JONES, SOPHOMORE

ds are white, fluffy dreams, fashioned by God.
CAROL JACKSON, SOPHOMOR

uds is not a melting pot of individuals. Instead it is a patt minds, each independent of the other, yet working together.
MILLARD MITCHELL, J

is the hieroglyphics of the sub-conscious mind.
DICK SAFLEY,

THE GARFIELD PEN

JUNE 1948

PROGRAM

- Music Department Faculty Trio
  Mr. Jeans, Miss Jonson, and Miss Stew
    1- Mozarts Trio
    2- Beethoven's Trio No IV

I-Coontz Boys Quartet
  Quincy Jones, Gus Robinson, Thomas A
    1- I Don't Know Why
    2- Dream

II-Chalice Bridges
  Accompanied by Marlene Soriano
    1- Czardas

V- Don Apeland
  Trumpet Solo "Sounds from the Hudso
  Accompanied by Helen Apeland

-- Coontz Girls Quartet
  Members of Miss Wik's Chorus

I- Scott Family Trio
  Robert, Evelyn and Gail Scott
    1- Andante---Gluck
    2- Norwegian Dance----Grieg

II-"Blue Dreams"
  Composed and Played by Quincy Jones

III-Chalice Bridges
  Accompanied by Malrene Soriano
  Sleeping Beauty Ballet

X- Coontz Swing Band with
  Coontz Girls and Boys Quartet
    1-To Each His Own
    2- Blue Skies
    3- Talk of the Town

-- Selections by German Band
  BoB Braendlein, Janet Patek, Gary
  Ken Williams

I- Barber Shop Quartet
  "Let Me Call You Sweetheart"
  ****COMMUNITY SING***

II- Coontz Jr. High School Band
    1-Blaze of Glory
    2-Balls across the Meadow
    3-Pan-American

ary Ayers, Doug Bartlett, Arlene Beauchamp,
russ Boettcher, Lola Buckley, Thomas, Adams,

Joseph Powe was my first music teacher. I babysat his kids for free when I was 11 so I could read his books on arranging and scoring. He was elegant and dignified—the way I thought we all should be when we grow up. ~ Q

SCHOOL DAYS

WHEN QUINCY WENT to Garfield High in the late 1940s, it was the most integrated high school in Seattle. Whites, Asians, African Americans—all were thrown into the same melting pot. When you make music for everyone, it sure helps to know all kinds one-to-one, as Jimi Hendrix would also find when he went to Garfield a decade later. Moving amidst the rainbow-colored student body helped lay the foundation for an easy mix in both musical and social orders that Quincy has put into action in his work and his life to this day. Garfield was also where he met his first wife, a white girl named Jeri Caldwell, at a time when such interracial relationships were rare.

"I never even thought about an interracial situation or anything; it just didn't have anything to do with that," she emphasized half a century later. "He had a very pleasant personality, and he had charisma." Quincy went as far as to declare his intention to marry Jeri at his first meeting with her mother, who urged her daughter to wait until graduation before seeing her boyfriend again. Jeri couldn't hold out, though, and would in several years become both his first wife and the mother of his first child.

High school gave Quincy his education in the basics of both love and learning, but his real education was taking place outside the classroom. Even before graduation, he was hitting both the bandstand and the textbooks,

performing as a pro in numerous local bands. "We played three jobs a night," he states with pride. "We played the white tennis club dinners, then we'd play the black clubs for strippers. We'd do comedy, dance, we'd play rhythm and blues, we'd have to play scottisches, Sousa, Debussy … and bar mitzvahs. We did it all, man. And I was happy about that."

Quincy also learned a valuable lesson from one of his youthful colleagues. "We used to try to make the schottisches sound like bebop, and Ray Charles always says, 'Let the music have its own soul,'" he remarks. "Those are great words of advice. Don't try to enforce your attitude on another soul. And I feel that way about different countries—and life—now, too."

Though Quincy won a music scholarship to Seattle University, he didn't find the courses interesting enough. A scholarship to Boston's Schillinger House would be his ticket out of Seattle, but he was quickly outgrowing any institution of higher learning. You can't resist the pull of the Big Apple when you're just a train ride away, and it wasn't long before Quincy was out of the classroom for good, and thrust into the center of the jazz universe in New York City.

opposite top right: Berklee College founder Larry Berk with Q.

RAY CHARLES

above: Q, not Ray!

top left: Q's Big Band with Ray Charles in 1971 on the *Merv Griffin Show*.

top right: Marquee c. 1983 for Q's fiftieth birthday.

opposite top: Q and Ray at Q's induction into the American Academy of Achievement in Minneapolis in 1984.

opposite bottom: Q and Ray in the "I'll Be Good to You" music video.

Shortly after Quincy's family moved from Bremerton to Seattle, he moseyed down to the Elks Club to check out a sixteen-year-old singer he'd heard about who'd just gotten into town. Just fourteen himself, Quincy was blown away by the blind singer who'd hopped on a bus from the faraway state of Florida to get as far away from his birthplace as he could without falling into the Pacific Ocean. And he wasn't just blown away by Ray Charles's music, though its mix of gospel and R&B would soon burn down its share of roadhouses. "When Ray first came to Seattle, he had two girlfriends, his own apartment—I'm still living at home—two suits, a record player. He was like a hundred years older than me, man!"

When you're just waking up to your own potential, it's a godsend to have a buddy around to show you some ropes, especially one who's already hurdled more and tougher obstacles than have ever been thrown in your path. If he can do it, so can you. "It was like somebody forgot to tell Ray he was blind," marveled Quincy. "In fact, Ray never acted blind until a pretty girl was around; then he'd get all helpless and sightless, bumping into walls and doors, trying to get laid. I'd often go by his place just to eat—he'd cook chicken in his kitchen with all the lights off and the shades down. We'd eat, and he'd sit at the piano and show me what he knew, and I ate it all up, everything, his fried chicken, his knowledge, his friendship. He even taught me in Braille. Ray was a role model at a time when I had few. He understood the world in ways I didn't."

Ray also understood that music was a gigantic gumbo to be stirred, not something to be stuck into different bags. In the early days, "Ray sang like Charles Brown and Nat Cole, and played alto sax like Charlie Parker, but by the time he got back from California he had reinvented himself, and was playing gospel. He refused to put limits on himself. We both loved bebop—Ray was so good he used to trade fours at the Jackson Street Elks Club with the great saxophonist Wardell Gray, and that was on sax—but Ray loved the blues, he liked country-and-western, he liked classical." And Charles wasn't afraid to take risks that might get dissed as foolish but would pay off big time in the long run, like the time "he bought a Wurlitzer piano and stuck it in his living room. It sounded tinny and thin. At first folks laughed at Ray's stupid little electric piano, but when he wrote a hit on it called 'What'd I Say,' no one laughed anymore."

One of Ray's greatest gifts to Quincy was giving him a language that could put the sounds buzzing around his head into something that could be made into living, breathing music, with more soul and dimension than anything the pair might cook up on their own, no matter how many instruments they'd mastered. "Ray, he opened my eyes to orchestration," says Quincy. "I was trying to unlock that magic door to what orchestration was all about. How do you get four trombones and four trumpets and five saxes playing the same song? And he explained how you key them. I had such a thirsty mind. I wanted to learn everything."

In the early 1950s, Quincy was playing in Lionel Hampton's band and Ray was playing in Lowell Fulson's band, but their paths would often cross. Q kept telling everybody, "Wait until you hear my man Six-Nine from Seattle." Though Quincy and Ray's paths parted when Jones left for the East Coast, you can't keep such brothers apart for too long. They'd soon reunite when Quincy applied some of Ray's lessons to the ultimate test: arranging some of Ray's best recordings of the late 1950s and early 1960s. They got both suave and tough on the 1960 album Genius + Soul=Jazz, featuring Charles's Top Ten instrumental "One Mint Julep." They continued to team up as the years rolled by for more special projects, like when Quincy scored the 1967 hit film In the Heat of the Night and co-wrote the eponymous theme song with Alan and Marilyn Bergman, which Ray sang. Keeping in mind Ray's refusal to set limits, Quincy also wrote an orchestral piece that Charles performed with the Houston

Symphony in the early '70s, "Black Requiem," described by Jones as a portrayal of "the struggle of the blacks in the United States from day one of the slave trip."

That's a long way from the Seattle clubs where Ray and Quincy first dug each other's vibe, but it was a trip they were determined to take, both in their own unique ways and, when the occasion presented itself, as a team. "Ray and I used to dream about all of the things that were almost impossible, that had never happened before," Quincy says. "Black composers for movies, which I wanted to do since I was fifteen. Symphony orchestras. It's ironic, because we ended up doing all of that. I wrote 'Black Requiem' for him; we did 'In the Heat of the Night' together, and 'I'll Be Good to You' with Chaka Khan. We did 'We Are the World' together. All of our dreams, we did together."

WHEN I WAS 15 YEARS OLD, EXCITED ABOUT JOINING THE LIONEL HAMPTON ORCHESTRA, MRS. HAMPTON SCREAMED, "GET THAT CHILD OFF OF THIS BAND BUS AND LET HIM FINISH HIS EDUCATION"

5 YEARS LATER ON A TRAIN LEAVING OSLO, NORWAY, MRS. HAMPTON SCREAMED "IF THEY WON'T LET MY PARROTS ON, THEN TAKE THE WHOLE BAND OFF" (P.S. WE GOT OFF, AND IT WAS COLD!!

THERE WAS ALWAYS A DEPTH & WARM GLOW OF ADMIRATION SURROUNDING THIS STRONG-WOMAN— I'LL NEVER FORGET HER STRENGTH—

LADY GLADYS HAMPTON, A PROUD LADY, WITH VISION WAY AHEAD OF HER TIME. FOR HER LOVED ONES, HER CO-WORKERS, AND HER BLACK BROTHERS & SISTERS. HER SPIRIT IN APPROACHING A DIFFICULT TASK WILL ALWAYS BE FELT IN ALL OF US AS SIGNIFICANT & PROGRESSIVE.

NANCY TONR

LIONEL HAMPTON

Vibraphonist and swing jazz great Lionel Hampton, notes Quincy, "wanted me to join his band when I was fifteen. I got on the band bus, 'cause I didn't want him to change his mind, or my parents to know. I sat there all day. So all the guys got on the bus, and his wife said, 'Lionel, what's that child doing on the bus?'" he laughs.

"He said, 'I just hired him.' She said, 'Come here, honey. Get off the bus. Go back to school. We'll talk to you later.' I've never been so upset or hurt in my life, 'cause that was my dream, to play with that band. That band was bigger than Louis Armstrong, Count Basie, Duke Ellington, all of them. Hampton and Louis Jordan were like the first rock-and-roll bands, back in the '40s." But it wasn't long after starting courses at Schillinger House in the early 1950s that a still teenaged Quincy got the call to be part Lionel Hampton's band. This time, with no family or school obligations to hold him back, he eagerly accepted.

Quincy might have thought he was prepared for the big time when he was fifteen, and even more so on the cusp of adulthood. But the demands of being in one of the biggest big bands were an even greater challenge than he was expecting, as Hampton "was relentless. He would not stop until he got that audience almost in a frenzy! Every night...there were no limitations at all. The old guys said, 'Be careful when you get happy one night and get some physical business going, because you'll have to do it every night. So you can't just do it and stop, because it's part of the show.' With the handclaps, we used to do that with the gloves that shine in the dark. It was show business. Hamp's was a show band; he had five singers and dancers and everything. I loved it."

Even in one of his first interviews back in 1954, Quincy knew his time with Lionel was something special. "The year and a half on the road with Hampton was worth ten years in experience," he told Downbeat. "I did a lot of watching, and I learned a lot." But you also had to look the part as well as play the part, even if it meant losing a little face in front of some of your other heroes, as he found out when his bandleader made him wear "a special outfit ... kind of purple shorts, and socks and shoes and purple coats, and Tyrolean hats! He was gonna make us wear this shit. When Hamp went upstairs, we followed behind him, and standing there were Miles, Charlie Mingus, Thelonious Monk, Bud Powell, Bird, all these hip dudes. Our idols, you know? You'd just be dying of shame to let these guys see us wearing this kind of shit, you know? So Clifford [Brown] and I ran back down the steps and started to act like we were tying our shoes. Because we couldn't do it. We were too humiliated ... You talk about conflict of styles."

HAMP'S NEW STAR—Quincy Jones Jr., composer and arranger, is one of Lionel Hampton's brightest new discoveries. A graduate of Seattle University, Jones won a scholarship to study the Schillinger System in Boston. On a recent tour of the East Hampton remembered Jones and signed him to play with his orchestra. Young Jones is very proficient on the trumpet and is composer of "From the Four Winds," a modern suite, and other numbers. The trumpet ace has gained much experience from his travels with Eckstine, Calloway, McShann and others. Jones' arrangements are among the best and in keeping with Hampton's imaginative musicianship.

top left: Anthony Ortega, Clifford Scott, Jimmy Cleveland, Q, and Oscar Estelle during their nightly performance of "Kingfish."

top right: Sitting L to R: Joyce Bryant, Lionel Hampton, Johnny Ray; Standing L to R: Gil Bernal, Billy May, Jimmy Scott, Junior Parker, Q, unidentified.

opposite, clockwise from top: Gladys Hampton.

Art Farmer, Q, Hamp (in background) and Walter "Suede" Williams.

Recording session with the Hampton Band.

Lionel's band was like my dream. It was designed to have the full range of serious music, entertainment, and show business. To me, Hamp was the first rock'n'roll band, concerned with having a big funky beat, and really seduced an audience with a passion, just like Louis Jordan and His Tympany Five. And on top of the big beat he would drag in swing music, bebop, or whatever felt good. It was truly like a traveling music University. ~ Q

Q in Stockholm, the Hampton Band's second European stop, after buying his first overcoat at the NK department store.

opposite left: Quincy's first look at Paris, with the Lionel Hampton Band (left to right) Buster Cooper and Clifford Soloman.

opposite right: Lionel Hampton Band arriving at the Palais d'Orsay train station and hotel in Paris in 1953.

EUROPEAN TOURS

SINCE JAZZ IS ONE of the great American art forms, and one that African Americans are primarily responsible for originating, it's a cruel irony that many black jazz musicians have had to travel to Europe to get the respect they deserve. Like all black jazz musicians of the 1950s, Quincy had run into his share of prejudice and getting treated as something less than a human being in the country of his birth. So he was pleased to find on his first visit to Europe that "it was very clear that they were treating [jazz] like a pure art form.

We were all shocked by it because Americans don't look at it like that. I guess they figure that if it was involving African Americans playing in a bordello, it can't be very important.

"I'll never forget one of the directors from ANTA, a political association, leaving us with the warm farewell message just before we got on the plane of 'I'd just like to remind YOU PEOPLE that you're over there representing the United States, and we are asking you to please indulge in your idiosyncrasies discretely.'"

Some of the biggest eye-openers that took him for a loop were during his groundbreaking tours around the globe, in 1953 with Hampton, and three years later as trumpeter, arranger, and musical

director of Dizzy Gillespie's band on the first such tour sponsored by the State Department. Taking bebop to Beirut, for instance, "was a shock. We arrived at the airport, and 3,000 people were waiting. We saw a government plane that resembled a smaller *Air Force One* en route to Israel swoop in and watched [Secretary of State] John Foster Dulles get out and stretch his legs. We thought this was his crowd, but they had come to greet *us*. Still, it was hot, funky, and tense. There was civil unrest going on, and no one could really guarantee our safety. We were a long way from home, a world away from what we knew, with folks fighting over matters we knew nothing about. When it came time to play the concert, there was no one who could outright say we'd be safe onstage, but Dizzy wouldn't hear of canceling it. He said, 'Fuck it, we're here to play,' and we did. Everywhere we went, there was tremendous love. The foreigners treated us better than our own."

Quincy ended up going back overseas a year later, during the summer of 1957, working as musical director, arranger, and conductor for the French jazz label Barclay Disques. But even as a young dude on the rise, he knew it would take more than the usual jazz chops to get as deep into music as he

wanted. There's a saying that American jazz musicians shack up with music first, then court and marry it later. So he also took advantage of his time in France to study composition with internationally renowned music teacher Nadia Boulanger, and started to dig classical composers such as Stravinsky and Ravel. He was catching on that his chief strength was arranging for a group of musicians not blowing his own horn, as "I always felt that the orchestra itself was my instrument. I had to make a commitment at some point, and I was more fearless with an arrangement than a horn. Clifford Brown, who used to occasionally dabble in arranging, and I jokingly made a deal one night in Malmö, Sweden—he said 'I'll play and you write.'"

It was time to put some of that woodshedding into practice, so as the '50s turned into the '60s, Quincy got an 18-piece orchestra (including his old mentor, Clark Terry, who, along with Quentin "Butter" Jackson, left Duke Ellington's band to join Quincy's) together for performances of the musical *Free and Easy* in Utrecht, Amsterdam, Brussels, and Paris. Then it was time to climb a more golden set of stairs, taking the big band on the road in Europe for ten months in 1960. It doesn't get much

I n the '40s, a lot of the guys
I copied Miles because you
couldn't copy Dizzy—his range
was too high and he played far
too fast. He was the musical and
visual personification of bebop:
his black beret, horn-rimmed
glasses, mustache, and goatee. I
had loved Dizzy ever since I was
twelve years old. He had style,
soul, wit, technique, substance.
He was like a leprechaun, with
the thick glasses, the cheeks and
neck that bloated like a frog's face
when he played, the bent bell of
his trumpet, the suspenders and
hats he wore. He was also one of
the funniest, most generous men
I've ever known. ~ Q

top: The Dizzy Gillespie trumpet section: L to R: Joe
Gordon, E.V. Perry, Dizzy, Carl "Bama" Warwick, & Q.

top right: Dizzy Gillespie Band in Karachi, Pakistan at
a local radio station. L to R: Diz, Q, Rod Levitt, Karachi
musicians. Q met Ravi Shankar and Chatur Lal for the
first time later that night.

At the Parthenon in Greece.

right: Gillespie and the band arriving from Turkey in
1956. From top: Rod Levitt, Q, Phil Woods, Lorraine and
Dizzy Gillespie.

opposite: Q's *Free and Easy* show band
in Paris, 1959.

better than that for a big band leader still a few years shy of thirty, but it also doesn't get much tougher than that when you're the guy trying to figure out how to get the paychecks paid, and the economic realities of keeping such a large ensemble going soon caught up with him.

"Surviving with my band over here has been a serious challenge," he confessed at the time, "We have no agent, no manager, and this is my first time doing this. There's so much organizing. I have 18 musicians to pay and a total of 33 people who are travelling with us to care about. When there's no work one day, I can't say as we would back home, 'OK, you'd better do some recording sessions today'—there just aren't any to do over here. ... I've lost $145,000 here in Europe. I've had to sacrifice royalties, and borrow, and do without so many things, to keep the whole thing going and pay everyone."

"I was ready to do myself in," Quincy eventually revealed. "I just couldn't handle the pressure any more. 'Cause it was performing, and payrolls, and trying to book, and everything else." The fulfillment of a dream was becoming an ongoing nightmare, the prospect of his traveling troupe getting stuck broke in Europe his biggest fear. Finally, in Turku, Finland, Quincy contemplated suicide—when all he really needed was some rest.

Feeling obligated to get the band back home to the United States, he sold his music publishing (later buying it back for almost ten times the sale price) and borrowed money from his old friend Irving Green against his royalties. Green also offered him a position at Mercury that, given his circumstances, Quincy couldn't turn down. The dream had ended, but another door had opened, leading to the next important chapter in his career.

Yet Quincy knows that just as every dream has its risks that can bring your world to a crash, every dream worth pursuing has its irreplaceable rewards. "I suppose I should have come home sooner, instead of keeping things going over there as long as I did," Quincy admitted not long after he came back to the United States. "But I'm not sorry that I didn't. I lost a great deal of money, but the band became the most popular band in Europe, and the experience was the kind of thing that only happens once in a lifetime."

I lost a great deal of money, but the band became the most popular band in Europe, and the experience was the kind of thing that only happens once in a lifetime. ~ Q

MENTORS

THOUGH HE'S NOW a major leader and role model in the entertainment industry, on his way up the ranks as a young man, Quincy Jones admired and learned from many mentors and heroes. The big band jazz musicians and composers he admired didn't just teach him the musical ropes; they also taught him about what it meant to take on a lot of responsibility and that to better yourself as a person is just as important as polishing your musical chops.

Clark Terry, Count Basie, Dizzy Gillespie, Miles Davis, Sarah Vaughan, Billy Eckstine, Nadia Boulanger, Billie Holiday's musical director Bobby Tucker "All these people have been there, and they put you on their shoulders to help you do your thing," Quincy's said. "It's very much appreciated because people don't have to do that, and most people don't, but they took me under their wing."

Sometimes the lessons were purely musical. For instance, "Dizzy was like a guru: He would sit and play the chord, the exact voicing on the piano, so you could get a very clear, illustrated understanding of what the brass section

was doing. He probably single-handedly introduced all the peripheral, related African influences into jazz, like Afro-Cuban, and he's always been willing to share that knowledge, to try to help to foster a new way of thinking about what jazz is all about."

And sometimes the guidance they gave could be tough love, like "one time Basie knew I was struggling with my band. He had too many gigs one night, and he let me have one of the jobs up in Connecticut at a dance hall. We went there and played, and the capacity was probably about 1,700 people. Only about seven or eight hundred people showed up. So when the man was paying [us] the money, Basie said, 'Give that man half the money back right now.' I said, 'What? Are you kidding? We have to pay these guys.' He said, 'Give him half the money back. He put your name up there for the best reasons, and you didn't draw. Don't punish him.' There are terms of ethics and fairness and so forth as a human being. Most people won't tell you the truth about that stuff."

top, clockwise from left: Bobby Tucker and Billie Holliday c. 1948 nine months after they worked together with the Bumps Blackwell Band at the Eagles Auditorium in Seattle

Q with Ella Fitzgerald.

Miles Davis during the recording session of *Back on the Block*.

Duke Ellington. Inscription reads in part, "To my friend, the great one who has decategorized the American Art— Quincy and his beautiful family. Good Luck, Duke 2/73"

opposite, clockwise from top left: Q with Count Basie.

Q at the foot of the master, Louis Armstrong, during their only collaboration—the song "Faith" from the musical *I Had a Ball*—which Q produced.

Producing and arranging for his "mentor and brother" Clark Terry c. 1955.

Q with Sarah Vaughan in Europe preparing another LP.

Duke Ellington on the set of *Duke, We Love You Madly*, one of Q's first TV productions that he did with Bud Yorkin and Norman Lear.

center: Q with Cannonball Adderley.

2

THE MUSIC
BUSINESS

I thought music could do it all. I had never thought about that [the music business] before, because we come from bebop, and we never thought about money or fame. EVER. Because our idols were on another planet; they had no concept whatsoever of money and fame. ~ Q

THE MUSIC BUSINESS

YOU'D THINK THAT ten years of arranging, composing, playing about as many instruments as there are fingers on your hands, and leading and feeding big bands touring the breadth of Europe, would make you ready for any musical challenge that comes your way. That's not the case, as Quincy Jones found out with a shock when he started working as an artists-and-repertoire (A&R) man at Mercury Records in 1961. That sort of school doesn't have classrooms; learning takes place on the road and in the studio. But in a way, his education in the music *business*, and the way you make and sell records in particular, had just begun. Great art doesn't always mean big paydays, and the financial bath he'd taken while touring his big band in Europe had brought home the hard economic realities of trying to pull off grand musical ambitions where the sales returns weren't on par with the artistic excellence. That doesn't mean you can't do some of both; Quincy proved that by producing, composing, and arranging many fine records in the first half of the 1960s at Mercury. But he also knows

now that you have to accept, even embrace, the need to branch out beyond jazz into pop as a means of professional survival.

"We'd lost all this money being stranded in England with my big band," explains Quincy today. "Irving Green, the president at Mercury, said, 'Come on back and work for the company. You know about music, but you don't know anything about the music *business*.' And I didn't. I thought music could do it all. I had never thought about that before, because we come from bebop, and we never thought about money or fame. *Ever.* Because our idols were on another planet; they had no concept whatsoever of money or fame."

Though most of his work in his first decade as a pro had been with African-American jazz musicians, Quincy's never one to bow down to musical and racial borders and, after accepting a challenge, moved into mainstream pop and rock by producing eighteen Top Forty hits for Lesley Gore. Just because you have to pay more attention to the bottom line, however, doesn't mean you have to sell

previous page: Rehearsing in Yugoslavia and trying to figure out how to convert dinars to marks so we could get to our next gig.

right: At work, on his first day job at Mercury.

opposite: With Floyd Standifer.

TIPS FOR SUCCESS IN RECORD BUSINESS

There's twelve notes, that's all. And Nadia Boulanger says, learn what everybody's done with those twelve notes, 'cause they're the same notes. Until there's thirteen of them, learn what everybody's done with all of them.

What I tell the young musicians is how important it is to be in control of your musical destiny. There's been so much loss of young talent in the hip-hop world: I can't get used to the idea of so many young people half my age passing away. Rappers have no choice but to be more responsible, but in order to do that, they have to live longer than twenty-five years. It's the first thirty years that are the hardest!

A band has to have energy fed to it. Its style has to be consistent with the ability of its sidemen. The spirit must remain stationary, even if there are frequent changes. Musically, you gotta believe, you gotta feel everything you do. To say you're gonna be commercial is not enough, because if you're not involved with a passion, an energy of totally believing what you're into, the essence won't be there.

out. Gore's records remain among the finest pop diva hits of the 1960s, and gave Quincy enough continued clout to keep producing less commercial outings by artists he loved who weren't gaining as much airplay in the rock'n'roll era. Thanks to the hits ringing up Mercury's cash registers, he was able to keep sharing the studio with great jazz singers like Sarah Vaughan, Peggy Lee, and Ella Fitzgerald, whose work has an aura of timelessness no matter what the decade. That still left time to pursue passions that couldn't be chained to any desk job, including making jazz records under his own name; arranging and conducting an album bringing Frank Sinatra together with Count Basie; and making his first forays into scoring films.

Producing such a diverse roster needs love, thoughtful planning, and a deft balancing act of musical and organizational skills. "When you're planning a record, the first thing you have to do is find the right song—which is key—then decide on a direction, a tempo, a mood—or a variety of moods," he told Max Jones in the 1960s. "You consider the artist's vocal range, catalogue, and repertoire, what he's made in the past. After that, it's mostly intuitive ... My part, as producer, is to try to be responsible for the final thing you hear on the record. Sometimes I have to bend the circumstances to make the overall effect successful. I like to step back and be the seeing-eye dog for everybody on the date.

"That takes a totally different feel and agenda than when you're working onstage. You really have to listen to what's going on from all angles, putting yourselves in the shoes of every singer and player on the field. When you're directing and leading a band, your point of view is one-sided. You're not in a position to hear the overall thing, your job is to straighten all the music out. But when that live studio sound hits that microphone, something happens to it. Believe me, there's a difference. Oh, man, many times I've had to completely re-orchestrate pieces to get them right for recording."

Quincy's produced many kinds of records, but whether he's doing a movie score, a jazz date, or a shake-your-booty funk hit, he knows the key to the jewel box is simply getting the best out of your musicians. The studio turns into a kind of workshop where you can't just play the right notes; you also have to get to know each other's strengths and weaknesses as *people*, not just players. "The biggest difficulty of recording is to be able to get straight to the truth real quick, because a band has worked that out on the road, getting mad with each other, and not speaking to each other for two weeks, and getting drunk together and everything," he made a point of noting when he was riding high as producer of disco-funksters the Brothers Johnson. "And in a sense, that's what

starts to happen with the guys you've worked with a lot in the studio over the years. You get to know exactly what their affinities are musically, and it's a real communication with each other.

"I can sit there and just write down every note and nail everything to the ground, and it gets that stiff, contrived sound ... it's not real, you know. So I go into the studio with a vision of what I want it to sound like and still leave room in case we get into a groove that's better. That's the magic you love. When you finally get it in the pocket, that's the nicest part of it all—that's when space is left for God to walk through the studio."

In the early '80s, Quincy made his most popular records—well, actually, some of the most popular records by anyone—as producer of Michael Jackson's *Off the Wall, Bad,* and *Thriller,* the latter of which remains the best-selling album of all time. But in Quincy's mind, what he does to shape such pop landmarks isn't all that different from what he'd been doing for decades with a passel of jazz greats. "Even in Michael Jackson's records, I was always trying to subconsciously force-feed the concept of jazz to the audience," is how he looks back on it now. "If you strip down Rod Temperton's song 'Baby Be Mine' from *Thriller,* that's stone cold Coltrane," breaking off to scat a bit of a jazz tune as an illustration.

Quincy's worldview embraces music of all kinds. In the end, it's all about quality, not classification. Good music is good music, no matter what you're playing, composing, or arranging, and no matter how young or old the musicians you're overseeing. It's a lesson he's put into action his entire career, and one he sees rooted in the spirit of Duke Ellington and other jazz and classical masters. "Nadia observed that there's only twelve notes in music. I love Duke Ellington, Charlie Parker, Miles Davis, Sarah Vaughan; I love Stravinsky, Stockhausen, Ravel, Alban Berg, Melle Mel, and Common. One of the proudest possessions I have is a photograph from Duke Ellington before he died. He wrote, 'To my friend, the great one who has decategorized the American Art—Quincy and and his beautiful family. Good Luck. Duke 2/73.' I hope I never let him down."

top left: Arranging and conducting in the Barclay Studio on Avenue Hoche with Henri Salvador and Eddie Barclay.

top right: Winning his first Grammy for "I Can't Stop Loving You." During the same year that a 21-year-old Barbra Streisand won her first Grammy. L to R: Q, Jack Jones, Steve Lawrence, Barbra Streisand, Edie Gormé, Tony Bennett, and Count Basie.

opposite: Q conducting Harry Arnold's Swedish Radio Band featuring Arne Domnerus, recording Q's song "The Midnight Sun Will Never Set," which outsold Elvis at the time in Sweden.

The Award Winning 18 Piece Orchestra OF

QUINCY JONES

DECEMBER 16, 17, 18,

THE EXCITING BIG BAND OF

MAYNARD FERGUSON

DECEMBER 23, 24, 25 and DECEMBER 30, 31
CHRISTMAS EVE MATTINEE and JANUARY 1st

CHRISTMAS and NEW YEARS
MAKE YOUR RESERVATIONS
►•◄ EARLY ►•◄

clockwise from top: The Quincy Jones Band on tour in Europe.

The Billy Eckstine show at the Apollo featuring the Quincy Jones Band, Freda Payne, Nipsey Russell, Coles & Atkins, and the Four Tops singing backup for Billy Eckstine in the same year that "Baby I Need Your Loving" went to #1.

"Back in America after being stranded in Europe for 10 months—we became the house band at Basin Street East with Eckstine, Don Rickles, Peggy Lee, and Johnny Ray."

opposite: Recording session of "Birth of a Band" at the Great Northern Hotel on 57th Street.

BIG BAND RHY...

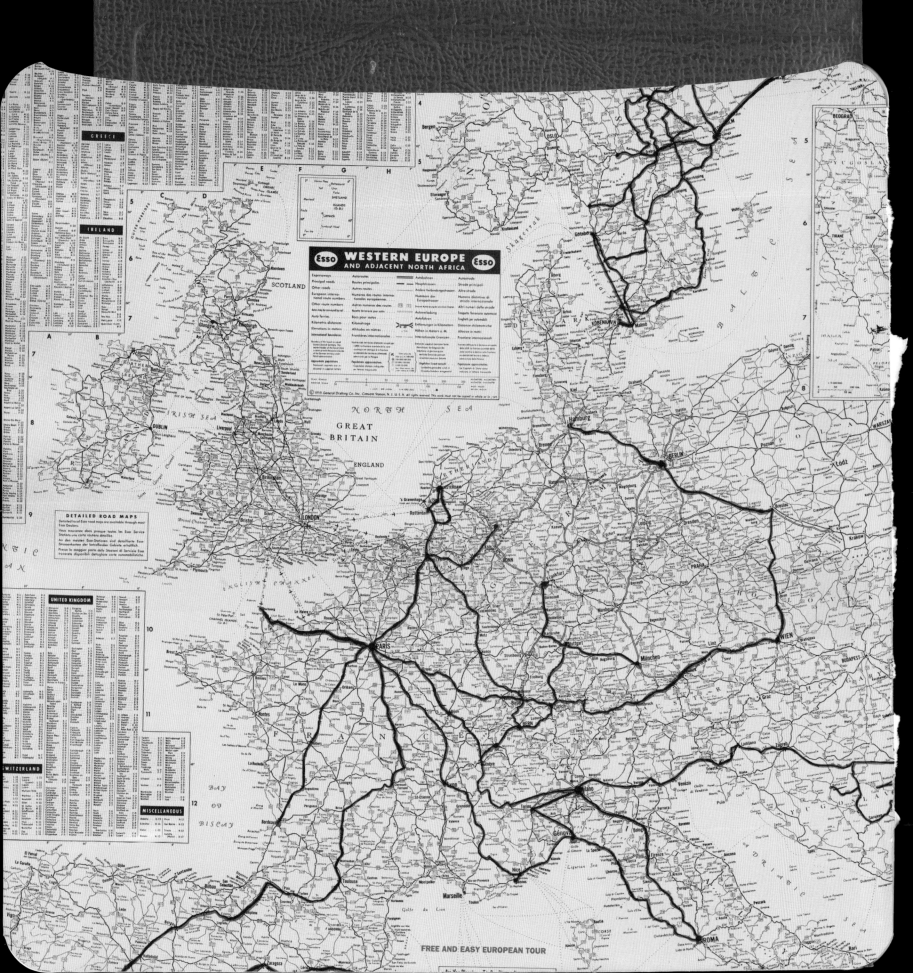

Music has been my touchstone because it instilled in me the belief in myself, which is the rarest of gifts, like a hard and brilliant diamond held in the deepest recesses of the heart. Creativity stoked my belief that I could shape my world, that I could find a place in which to grow up. ~ Q

MERCURY RECORDS

TAKING A BIG BAND through Europe is a blast, but it can also blow a big hole in your bank account. By the end of 1960, Quincy was more than $145,000 in debt after ten months of taking his entourage across the continent, shouldering both the onstage conducting and offstage responsibility for nearly twenty musicians. It would take seven years to climb out of that hole, and he might not have made it if Irving Green hadn't thrown him a lifeline by offering him a position at Mercury. But after you've lived the hardworking but freewheeling life of a performing and recording jazz musician for ten years, it's not a change that's easy to make overnight. "I was behind that desk every day," he's groaned. "Awful! You had to be in there at nine o'clock, and you had to wear these Italian suits. You had to fill out expense reports and all that kind of stuff. That really made my skin crawl."

But with a young family to feed and something to prove to an industry that was giving few such chances to African Americans, it was worth the sacrifice. Just as Quincy had hit the road and traveled the globe as a musician and bandleader, now it was time to fly the

world in h[...]st a quarter [...]

Jazz w[...] knew best [...] over a stel[...] Never one[...] heritage, [...]s and ment[...] Gillespie, [...] one to tu[...] he also re[...]n cutting-e[...] Roland K[...] for his mind[...]ral horns at[...]jazz icons w[...]e ones sel[...]ot to the te[...] rule the[...]ncy began f[...]ith someth[...]

"Th[...]y had [hitma[...]ens, The A[...]he recalls[...]loing Nina S[...]nita Jo, Di[...] stuff—[...]d an album[...]called *French*[...] 1,100

Named 'Veep' For Mercury

QUINCY JONES
... kicked upstairs

Multi-talented Quincy Jones has taken another step up the ladder of success in the music field.

Formerly Mercury Records A & R Director, Jones was recently named vice president of Mercury Records. This position is reputed to be a "first" for a Negro in the recording industry.

Called a "musical genius," Jones is former band leader. He is also a brilliant arranger, composer and all-around man musically.

He has arranged and composed for such great singers as Frank Sinatra, Sammy Davis Jr., Ella Fitzgerald, Peggy Lee, Ray Charles and Andy Williams.

Jones was the musical director-conductor for the Frank Sinatra and Count Basie Band during their sensational stint in Las Vegas.

Mercury Record Corporation

35 EAST WACKER DRIVE, CHICAGO 1, ILLINOIS
TELEPHONE: DEARBORN 2-5788
CABLE ADDRESS: "MERREC"

January 27, 1961

Mr. Quincy Jones
55 West 92 Street
New York, New York

Dear Quincy:

Mr. Green suggested that I send you the enclosed proof of an ad which will appear in the February 2nd issue of Jet Magazine. It was taken after we were told that you ranked Number One Composer-Arranger in their first annual jazz poll.

Sincerely,

MERCURY RECORD CORPORATION

Millie Stergis

M. A. Stergis
Advertising Administrator

P.S. I just received advance copies of the issue, and am enclosing one.

MAS/bk

Founded in 1947 on a Sound Basis

top left: Harry Arnold Swedish Radio Band.

top right: With Mercury's international director and inventor, Brice Somers.

LESLEY GORE

"It's My Party," was just the first of a series that are right up there with Phil Spector's girl-group hits as some of the most sophisticated, elaborately arranged pop-rock records of the era—"She's a Fool," "Maybe I Know," and the proto-feminist anthem "You Don't Own Me," ultra-catchy music that swings as well as purrs, and caused teenage hearts to fall in love with Lesley's ingratiatingly youthful, sincere vocals.

But the lessons of jazz are not always applicable to records made to roar out of car radios. Making a good, commercial pop record "turned out to be harder than I thought, plowing through piles of demo tapes, listening to bad singers do awful songs, trolling my way through garbage," he confessed many years later. It was also a matter of finding the right artist, not just the right song, and Lesley Gore "had a mellow, distinctive voice and sang in tune, which a lot of grown-up rock'n'roll singers couldn't do."

copies," he laughs. "And they said, 'Why don't you do something with the bottom line and come out with some hits?'

"It was a challenge, really. We had a meeting in Chicago, and they were slinging this cassette around, and I grabbed it 'cause I liked the sound. She was sixteen years old, and [agent] Joe Glaser came up to the office with her mother and father and said, 'I want her to have a #1 record,' like you can do it just like that. And we went on a Saturday and recorded it, and Paul Anka gave me a song called 'Danny' for the B-side."

The singer was Lesley Gore, and the record, "It's My Party," would vault Quincy into a new league at Mercury. Just after Lesley's recording session, Quincy went "late that afternoon to Carnegie Hall, 'cause I was recording Charles Aznavour. I ran into Phil Spector getting out of a limousine, and Spector said he'd just cut a smash with the Crystals called 'It's My Party.' I said, 'Oh my God,' and I freaked. But then I ran inside to say a quick 'Bonjour and goodbye' to Aznavour and rushed back to Bell studios to press up 100 acetates,

and we shipped 'em out to the [disc] jockeys," although Quincy had second thoughts about billing the single to "Lesley Gore," thinking she should change her last name for her professional work. That these two producers had independently discovered the same song was a fluke, but Quincy's quick work in getting his version out first paid off: Spector's was never finished nor released.

"I go to Japan after that to do a score for a TV show, and act in it with a big, famous soap opera character," Quincy adds. "Irving Green called me and said, 'You still don't like Lesley's name?' I said, 'Yeah, I still have a problem with it.' He said, while laughing over the phone, 'Just bring your butt home so we can get an album out!' We had 18 hits with Lesley."

Just as monumentally, Quincy Jones was now at the top of the hit parade in his own business with his promotion to vice president of A&R at Mercury. That made him the first African-American executive at a white-owned record company. And that's a milestone at least as important as any hit record.

It wasn't like standing still was bein' neutral.
Standing still was going backwards.
Standing still was impossible. ~ Q

Peggy Lee, with whom Q co-wrote songs and for whom he conducted and arranged recordings and live events.

opposite: With Leslie Gore holding their first gold record, "It's My Party."

DIVAS

A special nod to all the divas I love and have had the pleasure to work with in my career: Ernestine Anderson, Patti Austin, Erykah Badu, LaVerne Baker, Kathleen Battle, Ruth Brown, Kim Carnes, Diahann Carroll, Betty Carter, Petula Clark, Carmen Consoli, Mary Day, Céline Dion, Gloria Estefan, Ella Fitzgerald, Roberta Flack, Renée Fleming, Aretha Franklin, Siedah Garrett, Astrud Gilberto, Lesley Gore, Billie Holiday, Shirley Horn, Lena Horne, Lurlean Hunter, Janet Jackson, Damita Jo, Norah Jones, Alicia Keys, Chaka Khan, Angélique Kidjo, Peggy Lee, Big Maybelle, Letta Mbulu, Carmen McRae, Helen Merrill, Bette Midler, Nana Mouskouri, Jessye Norman, Anita O'Day, Karina Pasian, Freda Payne, Leontyne Price, Minnie Riperton, Annie Ross, Diana Ross, Hazel Scott, Nina Simone, Barbra Streisand, Riffat Sultana, Donna Summer, Tina Turner, Sarah Vaughan, Dionne Warwick, Dinah Washington, and Timi Yuro.

PRODUCING

QUINCY'S NEVER LOST his ear for a hit record, but neither has he lost his urge to honor the jazz stars who originally inspired him. That doesn't just mean showering them with praise and awards. It also means helping them keep on making living, breathing contemporary music, and not simply paying tribute to them as museum pieces. It may have been the Lesley Gore singles that were bringing in some of the biggest bread for Mercury during Quincy's time with the label, but he also spent much of his time there making sure that some of his favorite jazz legends could continue to cut albums that you could get at most record stores, not just in the cutout bin.

In a few cases, Quincy was able to give some serious payback by collaborating with stars who'd helped him get a foothold in the business in his younger days, like Dinah Washington, Dizzy Gillespie, and Billy Eckstine. Quincy's never been a predictable cat, though, and he also worked on some more unusual projects that might surprise even some of his devoted

fans. There was a Louis Armstrong album, cut shortly after Satchmo had topped the charts with "Hello, Dolly!" which included another hit adaptation of a Broadway theme, "Faith," from the musical *I Had a Ball*. There was an LP by pop-rock-soul singer Timi Yuro. There was even a gospel album by Little Richard, then easing his way back into the music biz after giving it up for religion.

In the record business, rising to a seat of power while leaving space for your pet projects can be a tightrope walk that's hard to pull off. One of the first hard knocks you learn in climbing the ladder is that it's not always going to be easy to keep doing what you want, especially when the balance sheet doesn't put art above commerce. There's even some derision from within your own ranks, as Quincy learned before his hits with Lesley Gore put a stop to it. "There were two guys on the Mercury A&R staff that were real musicians, Hal Mooney and myself," is how he's framed it. "And we always got jeered at because we were making records like

top left: New York session, correcting parts for Joe Wilder and Charlie Shavers.

top right: Recording and hanging with The Queen, Dinah Washington.

above: R to L: Sarah Vaughan, Q, and a friend.

opposite: Recording Sarah Vaughan's album *Vaughan with Voices* in Copenhagen with Robert Farnon (right side), one of the greatest string arrangers to ever live, and the Svend Saabye Choir. That's Sarah at the console in the center.

They offered me a million dollars to stay with the company for twenty years. I figured that was my whole life and my whole soul, and I really wanted to write for the movies. The music was calling. I couldn't stay behind a desk all day for twenty years. ~ Q

Julius Watkins with eight French horns, and Robert Farnon with Sarah Vaughan ... We'd sell, like, 1100 records. We really had to take a lot of shit at those A&R meetings. And I said making a pop record is not difficult, and they laughed at us again. So it was a challenge to keep the people that I loved; I saw that I had to generate some sales in some other place so we could keep the Sarah Vaughan thing going. And the first one we did with Lesley Gore did it."

Sarah Vaughan, the jazz diva known as "Sassy," has a particularly special place in Quincy's musical affections. He produced three albums for the singer at Mercury between 1963 and 1965. He takes pride in setting the groundwork for her to spread her wings and let her best self shine in the studio. "If I put her in the studio with a good song and a great arrangement, then Sarah is really free," is how he laid it out in 1963. "And that's what she likes. I've said that Sarah responds to arrangements. She's a very sensitive creature. Some singers have their thing and just blast ahead regardless of what's going on around them. But not Sarah. She uses her voice the way a great jazz musician plays his instrument. I'll tell you, a chick like Sarah makes it all worthwhile. She takes all the pain out of the business, makes up for all the

dues you've paid. The session will be a ball."

As sensitive as she could be in the studio, Quincy also knew about Sarah's truly Sassier side, which surfaced "in New York when we were all riding in a car to the Armory for a recording date I'd arranged for her with Count Basie. Sarah and the French composer Michel Legrand, whom I had just introduced, were in front; I was in the back. After a while, Sassy—who was a very introverted lady—lit up a joint and offered to share it with Michel—a gesture of the highest honor in the jazz world. Having just arrived and not yet streetwise, Michel rolled down the cab's window and threw the joint out. Sassy yelled, 'What's the matter with you, muthafucka? That's my shit!' All the French-American congeniality went out the window, too. What Michel couldn't have known was that after all those years on the road with the eighteen men of the Eckstine band, Sassy had learned to be one of the boys; she had to, like all the girl singers on the road, or her ass would have been grass."

Quincy always has several brainstorms going at once, and punching the clock at Mercury until he got his gold watch simply wasn't in the cards. Even when he was getting his paycheck from

the label, he kept on picking up some production and arrangement work outside Mercury. It's a good thing he did, as some of the outside projects benefiting from his helping hand were a couple early '60s Capitol LPs by Peggy Lee, as well as a couple mid-'60s albums by Frank Sinatra, one of which also brought Count Basie into the mix. From the outside, the VP slot at Mercury must have looked pretty good, as did a financial package that would have finally laid those demon debts to rest. But almost no sooner was Quincy in the vice-president's office than he left, "because I got tired of it. They offered me a million dollars to stay with the company for twenty years. I figured that was my whole life and my whole soul, and I really wanted to write for the movies. The music was calling. I couldn't stay behind a desk all day for twenty years."

That's not how most guys would react in that situation, but Quincy shifts stylistic gears more than just about anyone else of his generation. Unlike many of the artists he worked with during the Mercury years, he not only moved with the times, but he was one of the most creative forces in music's evolution, making it more electric and pop-R&B–minded in the 1970s, both on his own records and those he'd produce by the Brothers Johnson. Like similar moves by his friend Miles Davis,

these records are sometimes scorned by critics who'd like to see Jones, Davis, and others stay in the same bag in which they'd first made their mark. But since his late teens, Quincy has stayed well ahead of the curve, setting high standards, as he followed his passions, wherever they may have led him, instead of playing it safe. And one of those passions is funk, "because it represents basic, primal emotion reproduced bigger than life. I'm a cat that's into soul enzymes—I like someone who's emotionally committed to his music, and that could be Charlie Parker, John Coltrane, or Herbie Hancock. That *feeling* is the bottom line. That's all that's ever moved people. But, man, I hate seeing some cat plod along with the same two licks that were good 25 years ago."

top right: Quincy during the recording session of the song "Septembro," with Merv Warren looking over his shoulder. "This song was Sarah Vaughan's very last recording, God bless her."

The Brothers Johnson.

Aretha Franklin in 1972 right after Q and Aretha finished their recording "Hey Now Hey."

opposite top left: The Quincy Jones Band on a Norman Granz tour with Nat "King" Cole in Zurich, 1960.

opposite top right: George Benson studio session for *Back On The Block.*

opposite left: Nat "King" Cole on tour, with (L to R) Cookie, Maria, and seven-year-old Natalie.

FRANK SINATRA

When Frank Sinatra asks for your services, Quincy feels, you'd better drop everything for the job—no matter where, when, or in what unlikely circumstances that call might arrive. The first time he worked with Sinatra, "It was 1958. I was living in Paris, working for Barclay Records as a musical director and studying with Nadia Boulanger. We get a call one day that Mr. Sinatra would like me to bring our house band, which is 55 musicians, by train down to Monaco to play this sporting club for a benefit. We went down there and worked with Frank the first time. He was like a magician. I'd never seen anything like it in my life, the things he did.

"Only about six words passed [between us]. I didn't know if I was on his radar screen or not. And four years later, I get a call from Kauai. He was shooting a film, None But the Brave, and he said, 'Q'—I'd never been called that before—Bart Howard's song, "In Other

Words" [better known as "Fly Me to the Moon"], it's a waltz. I don't want to do it like that. I heard the one you did in 4/4; that's the way I want to do it. Would you consider doing an album with Basie and I?' And I said, 'Is the Pope a Catholic? Are you kidding?' I was over there so fast, and I worked with Frank from '63 until the day he died. Conducting Basie's band for Frank Sinatra—it doesn't get any better than that for an arranger."

It's a testament to Quincy's talent for getting along with all sorts of personalities that his professional and personal relationship with the notoriously mercurial Sinatra not only worked, but thrived. "Frank had no gray," Quincy adds. "He loves you, or he'd run over you in a Mack truck in reverse. He had nothing in the middle," he laughs. "Guys like Billy Eckstine, Ray Charles, and Frank Sinatra—you'd better be ready when you work with them, 'cause they watch you like a hawk. But I was ready for 'em."

VANITY FAIR: *When and where were you happiest?*
QUINCY JONES: *Conducting and arranging for Frank Sinatra and Count Basie at the age of thirty one.*

That was probably the most exciting engagement of my life.
~ FRANK SINATRA

top left: Frank and his goddaughter Martina Jones (six weeks old) at Nancy (Senior)'s home for a Christmas party in 1966.

top right: Basie and Frank recording "Fly Me to the Moon."

opposite, clockwise from top left: After the wrap of the film *None But the Brave* on Kauai, Q, Frank, and their posse went over to Honolulu for a couple nights of holy communion and holy water at a midnight mass to celebrate. Polaroid photos by Frank Sinatra.

With Frank, who presented Q the Scopus Award.

The first time Q met Sinatra in Monaco in 1958 at the Sporting Club. L to R: Eddie Barclay, Q, Sinatra

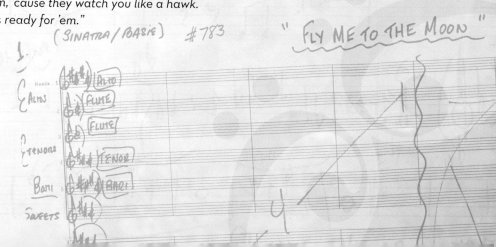

SOLO WORK

QUINCY JONES MIGHT be most famous as a producer of such albums as *Sinatra at the Sands* and *Thriller*, but don't underestimate both the quality and quantity of the records he's made under his own name. He started making those in the mid-1950s, and by 1960 had already snagged a Grammy nomination for *The Great Wide World of Quincy Jones* in the "Best Jazz Performance, Large Group" category. Others followed in the next three years for *I Dig Dancers*, *Quintessence*, *Quincy Jones Plays the Hip Hits*, and *Big Band Bossa Nova*. Ironically, his best-known track from that era remains the ticklishly frisky "Soul Bossa Nova," a piece he wrote in twenty minutes in 1962, and which featured the recording debut of Lalo Schifrin. Truth really is stranger than fiction— it's now an anthem of retro-fashion to an entirely new generation after its spectacular rise from the vaults, 35 years later, as the title theme for the *Austin Powers* trilogy and later went on to become a hip-hop hit, sampled in Ludacris' "#1 Spot."

Just as Quincy's not content to run in place as a producer, neither can he accept mining the same coal over and over as a solo artist. His move into funk-soul–flavored albums in the first half of the 1970s might have surprised the jazz establishment, but they also put his own work in the commercial mainstream for the first time. Albums such as *Walking in Space* (part of the genesis of black FM radio), *Gula Matari*, *Smackwater Jack*, and *Body Heat* scaled the upper reaches of the jazz and R&B charts, *Body Heat* crossing over to the pop Top Ten as well. His 1989 album *Back on the Block* garnered five Grammys.

It's a matter not just of being open to the changing sounds and times, thinks Quincy. You also have to be true to yourself, follow where your own changing tastes are taking you, and funnel those currents into your own vision. For example, the first of these albums, 1969's *Walking in Space*, "was the first time that I admitted to myself that I didn't dig only bebop rhythm sections anymore. I think electric bass and guitar turned everything around in terms of the rhythm section's function. That's what changed Miles's approach to soloing so much;

For a 2003 book and cover story called "A Century of Innovation," USA Today *asked*, "What was the technological innovation that most changed your life?" Q replied, "The Fender electric bass. Without it, there would be no Motown, no rock'n'roll."

he couldn't play the same lines over an electric rhythm section." (Quincy's arrangement for the song "Work of Art" by Art Farmer on the *Septet* album in 1953 had been the first to ever use a Fender bass.)

You also have to be eager to test and even break the shackles of the gigs that might be your bread and butter, as "when I did *Walking in Space*, I just wanted to get away from movies for a while—get away from the restrictions of synchronization and being locked up in a studio. I just wanted to paint a canvas that would have all of my favorite musicians on it and just sail, with no ropes to tie you to the ground."

Quincy took great delight in learning that this version of "Fly Me to the Moon" with Sinatra and Basie was the first song to be played by Buzz Aldrin on the moon. The song "Walking in Space" had come out the same year, 1969. In February 2008, Quincy was amused to find out that "Walking in Space" was still being played in outer space. "Last week I spoke on *The Tavis Smiley Show* to space with Leland Melvin, an astronaut on [the space shuttle] Atlantis," he proudly notes. "He took up 'Walking in Space' for his wakeup music every morning. ... Not a person in the world can plan something like that. It's insane. It makes you feel like you want to levitate." Coming full circle, Quincy has been invited to conduct "Fly Me to the Moon" with the National Symphony Orchestra during NASA's Fiftieth Anniversary Celebration near Washington, D.C., in September 2008.

opposite, top to bottom: *Back on the Block* recording session:

Take 6.

L to R: Melly Mel, Big Daddy Kane, Ice T.

Chaka Khan and Sarah Vaughan on a break from Sassy's singing "Septembro," her last recording.

The key to the mystery of a great artist is that for reasons unknown, he will give away his energies and his life just to make sure that just the right note follows another ... and leaves us with the feeling that something is right with the world. ~ Q

I hate people that say things like that—people that say, you know, "Quincy Jones should have stayed with jazz." Or whatever they say. To me, that shows that their viewpoint is in a box. The beauty of life is to be outside the box, so that the box doesn't exist. So that you have such a broader palette to work with, with expression. Music serves a purpose: expressing truth, expressing beauty, expressing reality, and also expressing dreams and hopes. And to limit it, to limit a human being to one mode of expression, is really a crime. ~ HERBIE HANCOCK

VISUAL DISCOGRAPHY

QUINCY JONES DISCOGRAPHY

SOLO ALBUMS

This Is How I Feel About Jazz (1956, ABC
  Paramount: ABC-149) (CP; AR)

Go West, Man (1957, ABC-Paramount:
  ABC-186) (PD)

Home Again (1958, Metronome: 1510)
  (AR; P; TRPT)

The Birth of a Band (1959, Mercury: MG-20444)
  (CP; AR)

The Great Wide World of Quincy Jones (1959,
  Mercury: SR-60221 (CD)

I Dig Dancers (1960, Mercury: SR-60612)
  (CD; CP; AR)

Around the World (1961, Mercury: PPS-6014)
  (CD; CP; AR)

Newport '61 (1961, Mercury: SR-60653)
  (CD; CP; AR)

The Great Wide World of Quincy Jones—
  Live (in Zurich!) (1961, Mercury: 195J-32)
  (CD; AR)

The Quintessence (1961, Impulse: A-11)
  (CD; CP; AR)

Big Band Bossa Nova (1962, Mercury:
  MG-20751) (CD; CP; AR)

Quincy Jones Plays the Hip Hits (1963, Mercury:
  SR-60799) (CD; AR)

Golden Boy (1964, Mercury: MG-20938) (CD;
  CP; AR)

I Had a Ball (1964, Mercury: MG-21022)
  (PD; AR)

Quincy Jones Explores the Music of Henry
  Mancini (1964, Mercury: MG-20863)
  (CD; AR)

Quincy Plays for Pussycats (1965, Mercury:
  MG-21050) (CD; AR)

Quincy's Got a Brand New Bag (1965, Mercury:
  MG-21063) (PD; CD; AR)

Walking in Space (1969, A&M: SP-3023)
  (CD; AR)

Gula Matari (1970, A&M: SP-3030)
  (CP; AR; CD)

Smokewater Jack (1971, A&M: SP-3037)
  (PD; CD; CP; AR; VO)

You've Got It Bad, Girl (1972, A&M: SP-3041)
  (PD; CD; CP; AR; VO)

Body Heat (1974, A&M: SP-3617)
  (PD; CD; CP; AR; VO)

Mellow Madness (1975, A&M: SP-4526)
  (PD; CD; CP; AR; KB; TRPT; VO)

I Heard That (1976, A&M: SP-3705)
  (PD; CD; CP; AR; KB; VO; TR; PT)

Roots (1977, A&M: SP-4626) (PD; CP; AR; CD)

Sounds...and Stuff Like That (1978, A&M:
  SP-4685) (PD; CD; AR)

Live at the Budokan (1981, A&M: AMP-28045)
  (PD; CD; CP; AR; KB)

The Dude (1981, A&M: SP-3721)
  (PD; CP; AR; VO)

The Birth of a Band—Vol. 2 (1984, Mercury: 195J-30)
  (CP; AR)

Back on the Block (1989, Qwest: 26020-1)
  (PD; CD; CP; AR; VO)

Q's Jook Joint (1995, Qwest: 45875)
  (PD; CD; CP; AR)

From Q with Love (1999, Qwest: 46490)
  (PD; CD; CP; AR)

The Quincy Jones-Sammy Nestico Orchestra:
  Basie and Beyond (2000, Qwest: 47792)
  (PD; CD; CP; AR)

SOUNDTRACKS

The Boy in the Tree (1961, Mercury-Sweden:
  EP-60338 (EP)) (CD; CP; AR)

The Pawnbroker (1964, Mercury: SR-61011)
  (PD; CD; CP; AR)

Mirage (1965, Mercury: MG-21025)
  (CD; CP; AR)

The Slender Thread (1966, Mercury: MG-21070)
  (CD; CP)

Walk, Don't Run (1966, Mainstream: S-6080)
  (CD; CP)

Enter Laughing (1967, Liberty: LOM-16004)
  (CD; CP)

In Cold Blood (1967, Colgems: COM-107)
  (CD; CP)

In the Heat of the Night (1967, United Artists:
  UAL-4160) (CD; CP)

The Deadly Affair (1967, Verve: V-8679-ST)
  (CD; CP)

For Love of Ivy (1968, ABC: ABCS-OC-7)
  (CD; CP)

Bob & Carol & Ted & Alice (1969, Bell: 1200)
  (PD; CD; AR; CP)

John and Mary (1969, A&M: SP-4230)
  (PD; CP; CD)

MacKenna's Gold (RCA Victor: LSP-4096
  (PD; CD; CP; AR)

The Italian Job (1969, Paramount: PAS-5007)
  (CD; CP)

The Lost Man (1969, Uni: 73060) (PD; CP)

Cactus Flower (1970, Bell: 1201)
  (PD; CD; CP; AR)

They Call Me Mister Tibbs! (1970, United Artists:
  UAS-5241) (PD; CD; CP)

Dollars (1971, Reprise: MS-2051)
  (PD; CD; CP; AR)

The Hot Rock (1972, Prophesy: SD-6055)
  (PD; CD; CP; AR)

The Wiz (1978, MCA: MCA2-14000)
  (PD; CD; CP; AR; AD; MS; KB)

The Color Purple (1985, Qwest: 25389-1)
  (PD; CD; CP; AR)

QUINCY JONES DISCOGRAPHY

VISUAL DISCOGRAPHY

ABBREVIATIONS:
PD: Producer • CD: Conductor •
CP: Composer • AR: Arranger • MS: Music
Supervisor • TRPT: Trumpet • VO: Vocal •
P: Piano • KB: Keyboards

SOLO ALBUMS

This Is How I Feel About Jazz (1956, ABC
 Paramount: ABC-149) (CP; AR)

Go West, Man (1957, ABC-Paramount:
 ABC-186) (PD)

Home Again (1958, Metronome: 1510)
 (AR; P; TRPT)

The Birth of a Band (1959, Mercury: MG-20444)
 (CP; AR)

The Great Wide World of Quincy Jones (1959,
 Mercury: SR-60221) (CD)

I Dig Dancers (1960, Mercury: SR-60612)
 (CD; CP; AR)

Around the World (1961, Mercury: PPS-6014)
 (CD; CP; AR)

Newport '61 (1961, Mercury: SR-60653)
 (CD; CP; AR)

*The Great Wide World of Quincy Jones—
 Live (in Zurich!)* (1961, Mercury: 195J-32)
 (CD; AR)

The Quintessence (1961, Impulse: A-11)
 (CD; CP; AR)

Big Band Bossa Nova (1962, Mercury:
 MG-20751) (CD; CP; AR)

Quincy Jones Plays the Hip Hits (1963, Mercury:
 SR-60799) (CD; AR)

Golden Boy (1964, Mercury: MG-20938) (CD;
 CP; AR)

I Had a Ball (1964, Mercury: MG-21022)
 (PD; AR)

*Quincy Jones Explores the Music of Henry
 Mancini* (1964, Mercury: MG-20863)
 (CD; AR)

Quincy Plays for Pussycats (1965, Mercury:
 MG-21050) (CD; AR)

Quincy's Got a Brand New Bag (1965, Mercury:
 MG-21063) (PD; CD; AR)

Walking in Space (1969, A&M: SP-3023)
 (CD; AR)

Gula Matari (1970, A&M: SP-3030)
 (CP; AR; CD)

Smokewater Jack (1971, A&M: SP-3037)
 (PD; CD; CP; AR; VO)

You've Got It Bad, Girl (1972, A&M: SP-3041)
 (PD; CD; CP; AR; VO)

Body Heat (1974, A&M: SP-3617)
 (PD; CD; CP; AR; VO)

Mellow Madness (1975, A&M: SP-4526)
 (PD; CD; CP; AR; KB; TRPT; VO)

I Heard That (1976, A&M: SP-3705)
 (PD; CD; CP; AR; KB; VO; TR; PT)

Roots (1977, A&M: SP-4626) (PD; CP; AR; CD)

Sounds...and Stuff Like That (1978, A&M:
 SP-4685) (PD; CD; AR)

Live at the Budokan (1981, A&M: AMP-28045)
 (PD; CD; CP; AR; KB)

The Dude (1981, A&M: SP-3721)
 (PD; CP; AR; VO)

The Birth of a Band—Vol 2 (1984, Mercury: 195J-30)
 (CP; AR)

Back on the Block (1989, Qwest: 26020-1)
 (PD; CD; CP; AR; VO)

Q's Jook Joint (1995, Qwest: 45875)
 (PD; CD; CP; AR)

From Q with Love (1999, Qwest: 46490)
 (PD; CD; CP; AR)

*The Quincy Jones-Sammy Nestico Orchestra:
 Basie and Beyond* (2000, Qwest: 47792)
 (PD; CD; CP; AR)

SOUNDTRACKS

The Boy in the Tree (1961, Mercury-Sweden:
 EP-60338 (EP)) (CD; CP; AR)

The Pawnbroker (1964, Mercury: SR-61011)
 (PD; CD; CP; AR)

Mirage (1965, Mercury: MG-21025)
 (CD; CP; AR)

The Slender Thread (1966, Mercury: MG-21070)
 (CD; CP)

Walk, Don't Run (1966, Mainstream: S-6080)
 (CD; CP)

Enter Laughing (1967, Liberty: LOM-16004)
 (CD; CP)

In Cold Blood (1967, Colgems: COM-107)
 (CD; CP)

In the Heat of the Night (1967, United Artists:
 UAL-4160) (CD; CP)

The Deadly Affair (1967, Verve: V-8679-ST)
 (CD; CP)

For Love of Ivy (1968, ABC: ABCS-OC-7)
 (CD; CP)

Bob & Carol & Ted & Alice (1969, Bell: 1200)
 (PD; CD; AR; CP)

John and Mary (1969, A&M: SP-4230)
 (PD; CP; CD)

MacKenna's Gold (RCA Victor: LSP-4096
 (PD; CD; CP; AR)

The Italian Job (1969, Paramount: PAS-5007)
 (CD; CP)

The Lost Man (1969, Uni: 73060) (PD; CP)

Cactus Flower (1970, Bell: 1201)
 (PD; CD; CP; AR)

They Call Me Mister Tibbs! (1970, United Artists:
 UAS-5241) (PD; CD; CP)

Dollars (1971, Reprise: MS-2051
 (PD; CD; CP; AR)

The Hot Rock (1972, Prophesy: SD-6055)
 (PD; CD; CP; AR)

The Wiz (1978, MCA: MCA2-14000)
 (PD; CD; CP; AR; AD; MS; KB)

The Color Purple (1985, Qwest: 25389-1)
 (PD; CD; CP; AR)

GENE KRUPA FEATURING ROY ELDRIDGE AND ANITA O'DAY:
Drummer Man (1956, Verve: MGV-2008) (AR)

HUBERT LAWS:
Hubert Laws–Quincy Jones–Chick Corea (1985, CBS Masterworks: M-39858) (CD)

PEGGY LEE:
Blues Cross Country (1961, Capitol: ST-1671) (CD; CP; AR)

If You Go (1961, Capitol: T-1630) (CD; AR)

LITTLE RICHARD:
It's Real (1961, Mercury: MG-20656) (CD; CP; AR)

HARRY LOOKOFSKY:
Miracle in Strings (1954, Epic: EG-7081 (EP)) (CP; AR)

The Hash Brown Sounds (1962, Philips: PHM-200-018) (PD)

ART MARDIGAN:
The Jazz School (1954, Wing: MGW-60002) (CP; AR)

CARMEN MCRAE:
Carmen/Carmen McRae (1972, Temponic: TB-29562) (CD; AR)

HELEN MERRILL:
Helen Merrill with Clifford Brown (1954, EmArcy: MG-36006) (AR)

You've Got a Date with the Blues (1959, Metrojazz: E-1010) (CD)

JAMES MOODY:
James Moody's Mood for Blues (1954, Prestige PrLP-198) (CP; AR)

Moody's Mood (1954, Prestige: PrLP-192 (10")) (CP; AR)

Wail, Moody, Wail (1955, Prestige: LP-7036) (CP; AR)

GERRY MULLIGAN:
Spring Is Sprung (1962, Philips: PHS-600-077) (PD)

JOE NEWMAN:
Happy Cats (1957, Coral: 57121) (AR)

Soft Swinging Jazz (1958, Coral: 57208) (AR)

Joe Newman Quintet at Count Basie's (1961, Mercury: SR-60696) (PD)

OSCAR PETTIFORD:
The New Oscar Pettiford Sextet (1951, Debut: DLP-8) (CP; AR)

Basically Duke (1954, Bethlehem: BCP-1019 (10")) (AR)

Oscar Pettiford (1954, Bethlehem: BCP-1003 (10")) (CP; AR)

The Finest of Oscar Pettiford (1955; Bethlehem: BCP-6007) (CP; AR)

BILLY PRESTON:
I Wrote a Simple Song (1971, A&M: 3507) (AR)

PAUL QUINICHETTE:
Moods (1954, EmArcy: MG-36003) (CP; AR)

RUFUS AND CHAKA:
Masterjam (1979, MCA: MCA-5103) (PD; CP)

AARON SACHS:
Aaron Sachs Quintette (1954, Bethlehem: BCP-1008 (10")) (CD; CP; AR)

BOBBY SCOTT:
Joyful Noises (1962, Mercury: MG-20701) (PD)

When the Feeling Hits You (1962, Mercury: SR-60767) (PD)

PAUL SIMON:
There Goes Rhymin' Simon (1973, CBS: 32280) (AR)

FRANK SINATRA:
It Might As Well Be Spring (1964, Reprise: FS-1012) (CD; AR)

Sinatra at the Sands (1966, Reprise: 1019) (CD; AR)

L.A. Is My Lady (1984, Qwest: 25145-1) (PD; CD; CP; AR)

RINGO STARR:
Sentimental Journey (1970, Apple: SW-3365) (AR)

SONNY STITT:
Sonny Stitt Plays Arrangements from the Pen of Quincy Jones (1955, Roost: LP-2204) (CD; CP; AR)

DONNA SUMMER:
Donna Summer (1982, Geffen: GHS-2005) (PD; CP; AR; VO)

BILLY TAYLOR:
My Fair Lady Loves Jazz (1957, ABC Paramount: ABC-177) (CD; AR)

CLARK TERRY:
Clark Terry (1955, EmArcy: MG-36007) (CP; AR)

Clark Terry in the P.M. (1955, EmArcy: EP-1-6108) (EP) (CP; AR)

THE THREE SOUNDS:
The Three Sounds Play Jazz on Broadway (1962, Mercury: MG-20776) (PD)

Some Like It Modern (1963, Mercury: SR-60839) (PD)

Live at the Living Room (1964, Mercury: MG-20921) (PD)

VARIOUS ARTISTS:
Save the Children (1973, Motown: M800-R2) (CD; AR)

The Official Music of the 23rd Olympiad in Los Angeles (1984, Columbia: BJS-39322) (PD; CP; AR)

SARAH VAUGHAN:
Vaughan and Violins (1958, Mercury: MG-20370) (CD; CP; AR)

You're Mine, You (1962, Roulette: R-52082) (CD; AR)

Sassy Swings the Tivoli (1963, Mercury: SR-60831) (CD)

Vaughan with Voices (1963, Mercury: MG-20882) (PD)

Viva! Vaughan (1964, Mercury: MG-20941) (PD)

Sarah Vaughan Sings the Mancini Songbook (1965, Mercury: MG-21009) (PD)

GEORGE WALLINGTON:
George Wallington Showcase (1954, Blue Note: BLP-5045 (10")) (CP; AR)

DINAH WASHINGTON:
For Those in Love (1955, Mercury: MG-36011) (CD; AR)

The Swingin' Miss D (1956, EmArcy: MG-36104) (CP; AR)

I Wanna Be Loved (1961, Mercury MG-20729) (CD; CP; AR)

Tears and Laughter (1961, Mercury: SR-60661) (PD; CD)

This Is My Story (Vol. 1 & 2) (1962, Mercury: SR-60765/60769) (CD)

The Queen and Quincy (1965, Mercury: SR-60928)

JULIUS WATKINS:
French Horns for My Lady (1960, Philips: PHM-200-001) (PD; AR)

ERNIE WATTS:
Chariots of Fire (1981, Qwest: QWS-3637) (PD; CP; AR)

JOSH WHITE:
At Town Hall (1961, Mercury: MG-20672) (PD)

ANDY WILLIAMS:
Under Paris Skies (1960, Cadence: CLP-3047) (CD; AR)

TIMI YURO:
The Amazing Timi Yuro (164, Wing: MG-20963) (PD)

NOTABLE SINGLES AND EPS ON WHICH QUINCY JONES APPEARS AS COMPOSER, CONDUCTOR, COMPOSER, AND/OR ARRANGER

ERNESTINE ANDERSON:
"After the Lights Go Down"/"Hurry, Hurry" (1962, Mercury: 71960) (PD)

LAVERN BAKER:
"Game of Love"/"Jim Dandy Got Married" (1957, Atlantic: 1136) (CD; AR)

"Learning to Love"/"Substitute" (1957, Atlantic: 1150) (CD; AR)

"Humpty Dumpty Heart"/"Love Me Right" (1957, Atlantic: 1176) (CD; AR)

BROOK BENTON:
"The Kentuckian Song" (1955, OKeh: 7058) (AR)

"Bring Me Love" (1956, OKeh: 7065) (AR)

THE CARDINALS:
"Near You"/"One Love" (1956, Atlantic: 1126) (AR)

THE CLOVERS:
"I-I-I Love You"/"So Young" (1957, Atlantic: 1139) (AR)

ARETHA FRANKLIN:
"Master of Eyes" (1973, Atlantic: 2941) (PD; CD; AR)

MARVIN HAMLISCH:
"If You Hadn't Left Me (Crying)"/"One" (1976, A&M: 1775-S) (PD; CD; AR)

LIONEL HAMPTON:
"Kingfish"/"Don't Flee the Scene Salty" (1951, MGM: 11227) (CP; AR; TRPT)

SHIRLEY HORN:
"For the Love of Ivy" (1968, ABC: 11108) (PD; CP; CD)

"If You Want Love (Main Theme from *A Dandy in Aspic*)"/"The Spell You Spin" (1968, Bell: B-727) (CD; CP; AR)

LENA HORNE:
Lena Horne: The Lady and Her Music (1981, Qwest: 3597) (PD)

RUSSELL JACQUET:
"They Tried"/"Port of Rico" (1953, Network) (AR; VO; TRPT)

KING PLEASURE:
"I'm Gone"/"You're Crying" (1954, Prestige 908) (CD; CP; AR)

"Don't Get Scared"/"Funk Junction" (1954, Prestige 913) (CD; CP; AR)

HENRI RENAUD:
"Meet Quincy Jones"/"Dillon"/"Wallington Special" (1954, Vogue (EP)) (AR)

JUNE RICHMOND:
"Sleep"/"Everybody's Doin' It"/"Devil and Deep Blue Sea"/"Between the Devil and the Deep Blue Sea" (1957, Barclay: EP-70105 (EP)) (CD; AR)

ANNIE ROSS:
"Jackie"/"The Song Is You" (1953, Metronome: B-647) (P)

HENRI SALVADOR:
"Blouse du Dentiste"/"Moi J'Prefere La March a Pied"/"Trompette D'Occasion"/"Tous Les Saints" (1958, Barclay: 70141 (EP)) (CD; AR)

THE TRENIERS:
"Say Hey (The Willie Mays Song)" (1954, OKeh: 9066) (CD; AR)

"Go! Go! Go!" (1954, OKeh: 9127) (CD; AR)

USA FOR AFRICA:
"We Are the World" (1985, Columbia: US2-05179 (12" single)) (PD; CD; AR)

CHUCK WILLIS:
"I Can Tell"/"One More Break" (1955, OKeh 7055)

"Search My Heart"/"Ring-Ding-Doo" (1955, OKeh 7062)

"Come on Home" (1955, OKeh 7067)

ARCHIVAL LIVE RECORDINGS

Swiss Radio Days Jazz Series, Vol. 1 (1994, TCB/Select Jazz 2012) (CD; AR; P; TRPT)

Q, Live in Paris Circa 1960 (1996, Qwest: 46190) (PD; CD; CP; AR)

NOTABLE QUINCY JONES CD COMPILATIONS

Pure Delight: The Essence of Quincy Jones and His Orchestra (1953-1964) (1995, Razor & Tie: 2088)

Greatest Hits (1996, A&M: 540556)

Jazz 'Round Midnight (1997, Polygram: 537702)

The Reel Quincy Jones (1999, Hip-O: 40168)

Quincy Jones's Finest Hour (2000, Verve: 490667)

Talkin' Verve (2001, Verve: 549540)

Q: The Music of Quincy Jones (2001, Rhino: R2-74363)

Ultimate Collection (2002, Hip-O: 585902)

Love, Q (2004, Hip-O: 000187202)

The Quincy Jones ABC/Mercury Big Band Jazz Sessions (2007, Mosaic: 5237)

NOTABLE COLLABORATIONS

w/ HARRY ARNOLD:
Harry Arnold + Big Band + Quincy Jones = Jazz! (1958, Metronome: MLP-15010) (CD; CP; AR)

w/ BILL COSBY:
Original Jam Sessions 1969 (2004, Concord Jazz: 2257) (PD)

w/ MILES DAVIS:
Miles & Quincy Live at Montreux (1991, Warner Bros.: 45221) (PD; CD)

w/ ART FARMER:
Quincy Jones and Swedish-American All-Stars (1953, Prestige: PrLP-172 (10")) (CD; CP; AR)

ON OTHER ARTISTS' RECORDS AS COMPOSER, CONDUCTOR, COMPOSER, AND/OR ARRANGER

CANNONBALL ADDERLEY:
Julian "Cannonball" Adderley (1955, EmArcy: MG-36043) (CD; CP; AR)

HERB ALPERT:
You Smile, the Song Begins (1974, A&M: 3620) (AR)

RAY ANTHONY:
Standards (1954, Capitol: T663) (AR)

LOUIS ARMSTRONG:
Louis (1964, Mercury: MG-61081) (AR)

PATTI AUSTIN:
Every Home Should Have One (1981, Qwest: QWS-3591) (PD; AR)

Patti Austin (1984, Qwest: 1-23974) (PD)

EDDIE BARCLAY:
Et Voilà (1957, Barclay: 82.138) (AR)

Twilight Time (1960, Barclay: SR-60167) (AR)

COUNT BASIE:
Basie—One More Time (1958, Roulette: SR-52024) (CP; AR)

Basie-Eckstine, Inc. (1959, Roulette: SR-52029) (AR)

String Along with Basie (1959, Roulette: R-52051) (CP; AR)

Li'l Ol' Groovemaker...Basie! (1963, Verve: V6-8549) (CD; CP; AR)

This Time by Basie: Hits of the '50s and '60s (1963, Reprise R-6070) (CD; AR)

TONY BENNETT:
The Movie Songs Album (1966, Columbia: CS-9272) (CD; CP; AR)

GEORGE BENSON:
Give Me the Night (1980, Qwest: HS-3453) (PD; AR)

BROOK BENTON:
There Goes That Song Again (1961, Mercury: MG-20673) (CD; AR)

BROTHERS JOHNSON:
Look Out for #1 (1976, A&M: SP-4567) (CD; CP; AR)

Right on Time (1977, A&M: SP-4644) (CD; CP; AR)

Blam (1978, A&M: SP-4685) (PD; AR; CP)

Light Up the Night (1980, A&M: SP-3716) (PD; AR; VO)

CLIFFORD BROWN/ART FARMER:
Stockholm Sweetnin' (1953, Metronome: MLP-15020) (CD; CP; AR)

RAY BROWN:
Harold Robbins Presents Music from The Adventurers (1970, Symbolic: SYS-9000) (PD; AR)

DAVID CARROLL:
Happy Feet (1964, Mercury: SR-60846) (PD)

DIAHANN CARROLL:
Diahann Carroll Sings Harold Arlen's Songs (1956, Victor: LPM-1467) (CD; AR)

BETTY CARTER:
Meet Betty Carter and Ray Bryant (1955, Epic: LN-3202) (CD; AR)

RAY CHARLES:
The Great Ray Charles (1956, Atlantic: SD-1259) (CP; AR)

The Genius of Ray Charles (1959, Atlantic: 1312) (AR)

Genius + Soul=Jazz (1960, Impulse: A-2) (AR)

A Message from the People (1972, Tangerine: ABCX-755/TRC) (CD; AR)

JIMMY CLEVELAND:
Introducing Jimmy Cleveland and His All-Stars (1955, EmArcy: MG-36066) (CD; CP; AR)

SAMMY DAVIS/COUNT BASIE:
One Shining Hour (1964, Verve: V6-8605) (CD; AR)

DOUBLE SIX OF PARIS:
The Double Six Meet Quincy Jones (1960, Columbia: FPX 188) (CD; CP; AR)

BILLY ECKSTINE:
Mr. B. in Paris with the Bobby Tucker Orchestra (1957, Barclay) (PD; CD; AR)

Billy Eckstine and Quincy Jones at Basin Street East (1961, Mercury: SR-60674) (PD; AR)

Don't Worry 'Bout Me (1962, Mercury: MG-20736) (PD)

The Golden Hits of Billy Eckstine (1963, Mercury: SR-60796) (PD)

The Modern Sounds of Mr. B. (1964, Mercury: SR-60916) (PD)

DON ELLIOTT:
A Musical Offering by Don Elliott (1955, ABC-Paramount: ABC-106) (CD; AR)

ART FARMER:
A. Farmer Septet Plays Arrangements of G. Gryce and Q. Jones (1953, Prestige: P-7031) (CP; AR; P)

Work of Art (1953, Prestige: PrLP-162 (10")) (CP; AR; P)

Last Night When We Were Young (1975, ABC Paramount: ABC-200) (CD; AR)

ROBERT FARNON:
The Sensuous Strings of Robert Farnon (1963, Philips: PHM-200-038) (PD)

Captain from Castile (1964, Philips: PHM-200-098) (PD)

ELLA FITZGERALD:
Ella and Basie (1963, Verve: MGV-4061) (CD; AR)

ARETHA FRANKLIN:
Hey Now Hey (The Other Side of the Sky) (1972, Atlantic: SD-7265) (PD; CD; AR)

TERRY GIBBS:
Terry Gibbs Plays Jewish Melodies in Jazztime (1963, Mercury: MG-20812) (PD)

DIZZY GILLESPIE:
Afro (1954, Norgran: MG N-1003) (TRPT)

Diz Big Band (1954, Verve: MGV-8178 (EP)) (TRPT)

Dizzy Gillespie: World Statesman (1956, Norgran: MG N-1084) (CP; AR; TRPT)

Dizzy in Greece (1956, Verve: MGV-8017) (CP; AR; TRPT)

Dizzy on the French Riviera (1962, Philips: PHM-200-048) (PD)

New Wave (1962, Philips: PHM-200-070) (PD)

JOE GORDON:
Introducing Joe Gordon (1954, EmArcy: MG-26046) (10")) (CP; AR)

LESLEY GORE:
I'll Cry If I Want To (1963, Mercury: MG-20805) (PD)

Boys, Boys, Boys (1964, Mercury: MG-20901) (PD)

Girl Talk (1964, Mercury: MG-20943) (PD)

California Nights (1967, Mercury: MG-61120) (PD)

Love Me By Name (1976, A&M: SP-4564) (PD; CD; AR; KB; VO)

GIGI GRYCE:
"Jazz Time Paris" Vol. 10 (1953, Vogue: LD173) (AR; CP; TRPT; P)

DONNY HATHAWAY:
Come Back, Charleston Blues (Soundtrack) (1972, Atco: SD-7010) (CP; MS)

ROY HAYNES:
Jazz Abroad (1956, EmArcy: MG-36083) (AR)

SHIRLEY HORN:
Shirley Horn with Horn (1963, Mercury: MG-20835) (PD; CD; AR)

LENA HORNE:
The Lady and Her Music—Live on Broadway (1981, Qwest: 2QW-3597) (PD)

LURLENE HUNTER:
Lonesome Go! (1955, RCA Victor: LPM-1151) (AR; CD)

JAMES INGRAM:
It's Your Night (1983, Qwest: 1-23970) (PD; CD; AR; P; VO)

Never Felt So Good (1986, Qwest: 1-25424) (PD)

JACKIE AND ROY:
Bits and Pieces (1957, ABC Paramount: ABC-163) (CD; AR)

MICHAEL JACKSON:
Off the Wall (1979, Epic: FE-35745) (PD; AR)

E.T. The Extra-Terrestrial (Soundtrack) (1982, MCA: MCA 70000) (PD)

Thriller (1982, Epic: QE-38112) (PD; CP; AR)

Bad (1987, Epic: OE-40600) (PD; AR)

MILT JACKSON:
Plenty, Plenty Soul (1957, Atlantic: 1269) (CP; AR)

The Ballad Artistry of Milt Jackson (1959, Atlantic: SD-1342) (CD; CP; AR)

ILLINOIS JACQUET:
Illinois Jacquet Flies Again (1959, Roulette: 97272) (CP; AR)

BOB JAMES:
Bold Conceptions (1962, Mercury: SR-60768) (PD)

DAMITA JO:
This One's for Me (1964, Mercury: MG-20818) (PD; CD)

J.J. JOHNSON:
Man and Boy (Soundtrack) (1971, Sussex: SXSB-7011) (PD; MS)

THAD JONES:
Mad Thad (1956, Period: SP1208) (CD; AR)

JONES BOYS:
The Jones Boys (1956, Period: SPL-1210) (CP; AR; FLH)

LOUIS JORDAN:
Somebody Up There Digs Me (Greatest Hits) (1956, Mercury: MG-20242) (PD; AR)

ROLAND KIRK:
Kirk in Copenhagen (1964, Mercury: 20894) (PD)

Q first met a twelve-year-old Stevie Wonder at the Apollo.

left: Q in pre-hiphop outfit, 1972

MICHAEL JACKSON

Quincy's constant reinvention of the way he approaches music and recording has helped many artists reinvent themselves. It's a risk, certainly, but one that can pay itself back in huge artistic and commercial dividends. His most famous waves of that wand are without a doubt the records he's produced for Michael Jackson. In the late 1970s, Off the Wall established Jackson as a solo superstar; 1982's Thriller, the best-selling album of all time, was an industry phenomenon almost beyond measure, with estimates of global sales ranging from 50 to 100 million. Yet the Jackson-Jones team so instrumental to their creation came together by mere chance, and the pair almost didn't have the chance to even begin their studio collaborations, in part because both were so determined to do something outside of what the industry expected.

Though Quincy and Michael had first met when Jackson was twelve, they didn't really get to know each other, he clarifies, until "Sidney Lumet called and asked me to do [the score for] The Wiz. Michael was twenty or something, and said, 'Could you help me find a producer? I want to do my solo album.' I said 'Michael, great, but not now, I don't want to hear about it, 'cause we have too much to do. We have Richard Pryor, Diana Ross, all these people to pre-record. You don't even have a song in the picture! I can get you a song in the picture.' And they put the scarecrow song, 'You Can't Win' in. He didn't have a song!"

Just as Quincy works in the studio by observing everything and everyone, likewise does he observe everything when he's working on the film set. Just as crucially, he's also quick to pick up on those same qualities in others. As work on The Wiz proceeded, continues Quincy, "I started to watch him. He knew everybody's dialog, everybody's dance steps, every song. He had to get up at five o'clock in the morning to put all those prosthetics on. And I started to see something in him. Everybody said Michael couldn't be any bigger. I started to see something in him where I started to think, 'Oh, yes he can! There's parts of him they haven't seen.'"

Won over, Quincy eventually told Michael, "'I'd like to take a shot at your album as producer.' He goes back and tells Epic [Records], they say, 'No way! Quincy Jones is too jazzy, he doesn't even know how to make a record with you.' Michael

top right: An outing to Universal Studios in 1982 after recording "The Girl Is Mine." Standing: Q, Paul McCartney, QD3. Seated: Rashida Jones, Stella McCartney, Kidada Jones, James McCartney. Standing on ground: Michael Jackson, Linda McCartney.

Accepting the Grammy for Thriller, 1983

"Thriller" (Rod Temperton) © 1982 Rodsongs (ASCAP)

left to right: Rod Temperton is the best songwriting partner in the world, according to Q, and an even better friend. His hits include "Thriller," "Off The Wall," "Boogie Nights," "Grooveline," "Give Me The Night," and many many more.

At the 1983 Grammys.

L to R: Kidada Jones, Michael Jackson, Steven Spielberg, George Lucas, Q at a Fourth of July picnic at Skywalker Ranch around the time of *Raiders of the Lost Ark*.

came back crying, he was so upset." Wiser heads eventually prevailed, and the Jones-produced *Off the Wall* rose to #3 in the pop charts while spawning two chart-topping singles, "Don't Stop 'Til You Get Enough" and "Rock with You."

With an artist as multi-faceted as Michael Jackson, you have to work on all parts of his art and personality when you're in the producer's chair. Along those lines, "We tried all kinds of things I'd learned over the years to help him with his artistic growth, like dropping keys just a minor third to give him flexibility and a more mature range in the upper and lower registers, and more than a few tempo changes. I also tried to steer him to songs with more depth, some of them about relationships. Seth Riggs, a leading vocal coach, gave him vigorous warm-up exercises to expand his top and bottom range by at least a fourth, which I desperately needed to get the vocal drama going."

It takes two to make such changes effective, and the singer appreciated Quincy's guidance, calling him "a musical visionary. He can look at a clean slate and add all the elements. I've learned a lot as far as musical substance is concerned. [Quincy] once said, 'You don't write the music, you let the music write itself.'" Quincy in turn is impressed by the singer's dedication in the studio: "I love the fact that he asks so much of himself. I'm the same way. We're both musical junkies. It's a drag to have just one junkie in the studio. You need a room full of junkies when you are making a record."

Even when you're working with a talent on the order of Michael Jackson, you can't stand back in awe. You have to keep things loose to cajole the goods out of the genius. Quincy often called Michael "Smelly" "because when he liked a piece of music or a certain beat, instead of calling it funky, he'd call it 'smelly jelly.'"

Once during the Thriller sessions "a healthy California girl walked by the front window of the studio, which was a two-way mirror facing the street, and pulled her dress up over her head. She was wearing absolutely nothing underneath ... I got an eyeful. ... We stood there gawking. We turned around and saw Michael, devoted Jehovah's Witness that he was, hiding behind the console."

But such hijinx don't come at the cost of efficiency. Thriller was completed for about half a million dollars, using three studios in a mere four months—a blink of an eye in twenty-first century superstar recording terms, though not all that out of line with early-1980s timetables. When the smoke cleared, Thriller topped the charts for an unbelievable 37 consecutive weeks in 1983, generating seven Top Ten singles—and there were only nine tracks on the album—including a couple more #1 smashes with "Beat It" and "Billie Jean."

Though the third and last album Quincy produced for Jackson, 1987's Bad, couldn't hope to match Thriller's otherworldly sales tallies, it didn't do too bad. "Michael wanted to sell 100 million," Quincy chuckles. "I said, 'Michael, I've been out here too long for you to try to convince me that 25 million is a bomb.'" But it's not a surprise that Michael wanted more; like Quincy, he wants not just the best from his projects, but more than what most people would consider possible.

PRESENTED TO QUINCY JONES TO COMMEMORATE WORLDWIDE SALES OF OVER 40 MILLION COPIES

Michael Jackson Thriller

Thriller is certified multi-diamond by the RIAA.

MICHAEL
JACKSON

OFF
THE
WALL

RIAA diamond-record
for *Off the Wall*.

**PRESENTED TO
QUINCY JONES
TO COMMEMORATE
THE SALE OF MORE THAN
10 MILLION COPIES OF
"OFF THE WALL"**

RIAA multi-diamond presentation for *Bad*.

Miles Davis was the Picasso of jazz. He could paint pictures with his music. ~ Q

MILES DAVIS

Quincy Jones and Miles Davis are two of the heaviest hitters of twentieth-century American music, and it was inevitable the two titans would meet early on in their careers, when both were still very much in the jazz mainstream—a current that both would take radical detours from as their work outgrew easy categorization. Quincy was just eighteen when he met Miles Davis at the Downbeat Club in New York. Miles "drifted behind me and whispered to a friend in a way he knew I would overhear, 'I was getting down last night with three of my freaks and heard some young muthafucka with Hamp on the radio trying to sound like me.' Oh, Lord—he was talking about a trumpet solo I'd taken on my first recorded song with Hamp's band, 'Kingfish,' which was getting a little airtime on the radio. I was paralyzed; I had no idea how to respond to Miles. That was his way of acknowledging me and that was fine, because Miles was our god, totally

untouchable and unapproachable. Miles truly did not give a shit, even when he was young and broke. Everyone knew that Miles always spoke his mind."

Yet though Miles did contribute to Quincy's 1989 album Back on the Block, the two titans didn't collaborate closely until shortly before Davis' death. That's when Quincy co-produced a 1991 concert in Montreux of some of the renowned music Miles had done with arranger Gil Evans on the classic late 1950s LPs Sketches of Spain and Porgy and Bess. Quincy had been at those sessions (and the one for Kind of Blue) at Columbia's famed 30th Street Studio.

Quincy and Montreux Jazz festival founder Claude Nobs "had been in Miles's apartment in New York negotiating the contract with several lawyers while the man himself was upstairs working on a rap project with Flavor Flav and a rap producer. Eventually Miles eased down and inched further and further to the center of

the room. Before we knew it, he had gotten exactly the deal he wanted, for video and TV rights, and control of his images on the poster. 'This is gonna be real expensive,' he told us. I said, 'But Dewey, all we need is a large orchestra.' To my great amusement, he insisted, 'Q, you understand—this shit is hard to play.' Conducting Gil's orchestrations for Miles was one of the most gratifying experiences in my career."

Like Quincy, Miles had reinvented himself relentlessly over the preceding decades, and "It was the first time Miles had played this music since he had recorded it in the late fifties; up to that point he had adamantly refused to look back, ever. In general, his musical philosophy did not encompass retrospection." Recordings from the concert were released as Miles & Quincy Live at Montreux—the final album that Miles ever did. He died three months later.

Rehearsing with Miles Davis in Montreux with a double orchestra, 1991.

COMPOSERS

As in most things in his life, when it comes to composers that Quincy admires and learns from, all categories are welcome. Jazz greats like Benny Carter, film scorers like Henry Mancini and Armando Trovaioli, and of course his classical mentor Nadia Boulanger—all have a place in Quincy's universe.

For all he's learned about composing from study and observation, however, as he emphasized in a 2007 interview with Ben Fong-Torres, some crucial ingredients in the recipe lie beyond the rulebook. "Melody is the only thing that doesn't have a technique," he states. "Counterpoint, retrograde inversion, harmony and all that stuff has rules. Melody doesn't have rules. Melody comes straight from God. There are certain elements of it that you learn about the power of octaves and fourths and fifths, why they are so strong, and the feminine and masculine parts of it and stuff, but that's bullshit. The whole thing comes from God, another power."

I was putting together the Q box set, and we wanted to have Cannonball Adderley's "The Song Is You," from 1955. It had Kenny Clark, Cannonball and his brother Nat, Jimmy Cleveland, all these heavyweight jazz guys and someone named John Williams on piano. I said, "That couldn't be John T." I dug up a picture: yes, that's him, playing bebop piano. ~ Q

Q, Marilyn and Alan Bergman, Henry Mancini (seated), and John Williams at a tribute for Mancini.

NADIA BOULANGER

From Boulanger, Quincy learned that to excel is not only a matter of hard work and technique, but also of drawing from all dimensions of your abilities, emotions, and sensitivities. In reaction to Quincy's calling Stravinsky, whom he had just met, a genius, Boulanger replied, "If you have to use the word 'genius,' it should be to describe someone who has attained the highest level of achievement that involves sensation, feeling, believing, attachment, and knowledge." Whether or not Boulanger would classify him as a genius, Quincy was an apt pupil, later reflecting how his teacher "said a person's music can never be more or less than they are as a human being. I've never forgotten that." It's a lesson he's applied not only to his compositions, but to all aspects of his work as a producer and musician.

3

FILM &
TELEVISION

To Q, for
a hundred
reasons to
my thanks and
my love —
Alex

When I hear the words "That's never been done,"
I feel like a lion being thrown some meat. These
words pique my interest immediately. ~ Q

FILM & TELEVISION

JUST AS QUINCY JONES moves as easily between musical boundaries as he does as a host greeting guests at a reception for royalty, so has he shifted back and forth from the stage and the studio to the silver screen, the small screen, and calling the shots *behind* the screens. Making records just wasn't enough to meet all of his interests, so he took his talents into film and television scoring. When *that* wasn't enough, he went into movie and TV production. In some ways, this nonstop multi-tasker was well prepped to make the dive into fields beyond performance and discs. By the mid-1960s, he'd worn as many hats—multi-instrumentalist musician, composer, arranger, producer, conductor, and even label executive—in the music world as there were pegs in the cloakroom. His fascination with the visual arts, however, predates not just his first film scores, but his entry into the music business itself.

"I wanted to do movies all my life," he says. "I waited from fifteen to thirty years old before I got a shot, and that was *The Pawnbroker*"—the 1965 film that marked Quincy's first big-budget American score (he had done *The Boy in the Tree*, a Swedish film, the previous year). "Lena Horne told him [her son-in-law, director Sidney Lumet] about my music, and he asked me to do it. And I did six movies with him."

Offers didn't automatically come flooding in once he'd completed *The Pawnbroker*. Almost every new field Quincy's entered has dealt him an unexpected setback as he learned to climb the ropes, and the film industry wasn't quite ready to hand out choice scoring jobs, especially single screen-scoring credit, to African Americans. But once the barrier had been broken and his talent become apparent, more offers came his way, soon becoming an avalanche, and he moved to Hollywood to make scoring his main gig. *The Slender Thread, In the Heat of the Night, In Cold Blood, The Italian Job, Bob & Carol & Ted & Alice, They Call Me Mister Tibbs!,*

previous page: Q in Spielberg's screening room at Amblin during the making of *The Color Purple.*

opposite: Alex Haley, author of *Roots.* Q met him at a party 17 years before he finished *Roots* and they immediately bonded for life on all fronts.

On the set, producing *The Color Purple.* "In this shot, Spielberg was gracious enough to let me co-direct a big scene. I got the chance to walk in his shoes."

and *The Anderson Tapes* were only some of the assignments that followed in the next five years or so. Almost as soon as he'd established himself as a leading movie musicman, he became an in-demand television scorer and theme composer as well, working on *Ironside, The Bill Cosby Show, Sanford and Son,* and *Roots.*

"I always wanted to write for film," is Quincy's take on what many saw as an unexpected career move. "I don't know what it was, because I was in art first. I used to paint and draw caricatures on the school paper. To this day when I'm thinking of extended pieces, I think of them in terms of doing a charcoal sketch first, then to pastel colors. The contour goes on first; the melody, tempo, countermelody, and the canvas follow. Then I go to oils when it really gets to be clear, when the blur stops. It's a correlation that I love. So I've always tried to paint pictures with the sounds. They're closely connected to a visual image and that's why I love movies so much."

When you move from jazz to pop, and from New York studios to Tinseltown, there are always going to be those who think you're selling out for the glitter and gold. Some critics thought Quincy should be spending more time getting back into the pure jazz with which he'd first made his name, not slaving away in backrooms pairing sounds to images in Hollywood productions. "I haven't forsaken my jazz roots," he insisted. "But I just don't want to be labeled as a jazz writer. I want to do all kinds of writing.

It's my calling and always has been a challenge."

And, as he pointed out, scoring films isn't a sellout, even if it does have its own artistic limits: You can still do your thing and even put in some of that pure jazz when the window opens. "I still sneak some of that bebop music in where I can. Films are just about the only big outlet left to jazz, with all the clubs closing. With films like *In Cold Blood* you can really go way out. But you can't put jazz into everything. You can't have Roland Kirk playing grunt flute in a love scene. Suppose you just keep playing jazz that nobody can understand, just to keep these critics happy. What will those critics do for you when you get to sixty-five and you've gone out of style even with the few cats that did dig you?"

Multifaceted talents being ingrained in Quincy's DNA, it's no surprise that he eventually got a little antsy, and eager to take on new challenges in both movies and TV. "Every five years or so, you feel the urge to shift gears," he confirmed after about a half decade of matching sound to motion. "Besides, just as I had earlier with the three-minute record restrictions, I became restless with the short forms, the episodic cues that are the essence of film writing. Aside from that, in films it's a very isolated thing. You hardly ever see the people you're involved with. Half the time you're in some basement by yourself dreaming up ways to find new colors for a score."

While Quincy was able to begin to satisfy some of his hunger for new horizons with his first TV production, a 1973 special honoring Duke Ellington, he was clearly anxious for even bigger fish to fry. From the late 1960s onward, he'd pepper his press interviews with plans for ambitious projects beyond the studio, concert arena, or film and television. He wanted to produce a stage show covering the whole history

of black music. He wanted to do a jazz musical. He wanted to write music for a film of the life of Martin Luther King, Jr., with a script by James Baldwin. He wanted to produce a movie based on 1860s abolitionist Mary Ellen Pleasant, who became the first black female millionaire. Although those particular projects didn't make it from drawing board to paper, stage, or screen at that time, several remain in development to this day; Quincy thrives on taking on the workload of several men. Still, he was ready when the right opportunities could make that journey from dream to reality, including scoring the first episode of the landmark television series *Roots* (which garnered him an Emmy); co-producing the feature film *The Color Purple*; and serving as co–executive producer on the *Fresh Prince of Bel-Air* and *MADtv* television programs; producing the 68th Annual Academy Awards in 1996, as well as other media enterprises.

The entertainment business doesn't make it easy for people who want to call the shots from every angle, especially minorities. But as Quincy sees it, locked doors are made to be broken down. "When I hear the words 'That's never been done,' I feel like a lion being thrown some meat. These words pique my interest immediately."

top: Ray Charles and Bill Cosby.

Bill Cosby with Q during the recording session of "Hikky-Burr."

opposite top to bottom: Q co-executive produced the show *The Fresh Prince of Bel-Air*.

Q also composed the music for *Sanford and Son* and *The Bill Cosby Show* among many show themes he wrote over the years.

Cameo appearance in *The Wiz*, which Q scored and for which he was the musical director.

FILMS QUINCY HAS
SCORED TO DATE

1961: *The Boy in the Tree*
1965: *The Pawnbroker*
1965: *Mirage*
1965: *The Slender Thread*
1966: *Walk, Don't Run*
1967: *The Deadly Affair*
1967: *Enter Laughing*
1967: *Banning*
1967: *In the Heat of the Night*
1967: *In Cold Blood*
1968: *The Split*
1968: *The Hell with Heroes*
1968: *For Love of Ivy*
1968: *A Dandy in Aspic*
1969: *MacKenna's Gold*
1969: *The Italian Job*
1969: *The Lost Man*
1969: *Bob & Carol & Ted & Alice*
1969: *Cactus Flower*
1969: *John and Mary*
1969: *Honky*
1970: *Last of the Mobile Hot-Shots*
1970: *The Out-of-Towners*
1970: *They Call Me Mister Tibbs!*
1971: *The Anderson Tapes*
1971: *Brother John*
1971: *$ (aka Dollars)*
1972: *The New Centurions*
1972: *The Hot Rock*
1972: *The Getaway*
1972: *Come Back Charleston Blue*
1972: *Man and Boy*
1978: *The Wiz*
1985: *The Color Purple*
1990: *Listen Up: The Lives of
Quincy Jones*
2005: *Get Rich or Die Trying*

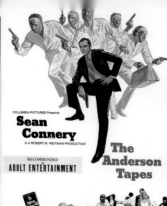

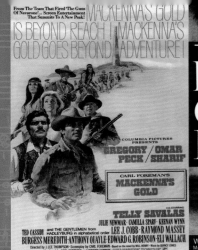
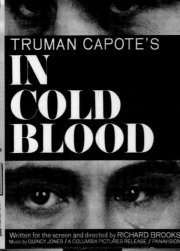

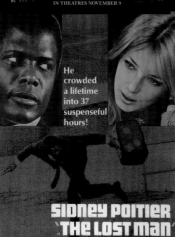

FILM SCORING

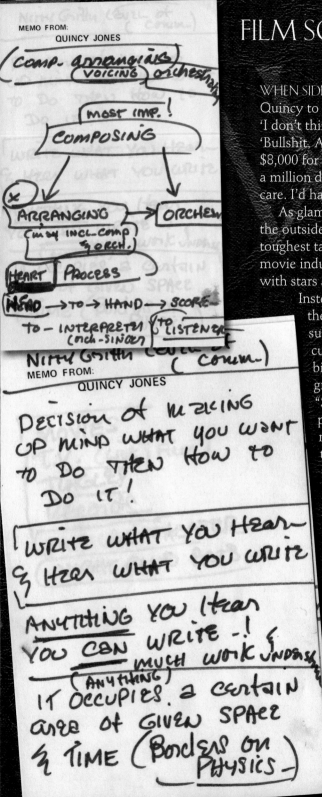

MEMO FROM:
QUINCY JONES

WHEN SIDNEY LUMET first approached Quincy to score *The Pawnbroker*, "I said, 'I don't think it needs music.' He said, 'Bullshit. And you're doing it.' I got $8,000 for that movie. Cats are getting a million dollars a movie now. I didn't care. I'd have paid *him*."

As glamorous as it might look from the outside, film scoring is one of the toughest tasks in either the music or the movie industry. You're not hanging out with stars all the time by any means. Instead, you're sweating through the laborious paces of making sure an endless number of cues, intros, and other musical bits and pieces make the grade for scene after scene. "Scoring is a multifaceted process, an abstract combination of science and soul: the psychology of scoring is totally subjective, reactive, and highly personal," Quincy feels. "The science is the technical process of synchronization. The soul is the process of painting the psyche with musical 'emotion lotion,' of finding the appropriate voice and tone for a film. Above all, the music has to sound organic to the subject matter or even sometimes in direct contrast to the subject matter while

accommodating a sequence of scenes that may be interiors, exteriors, medium shots, close-ups, quick seven-second shots à la *Star Wars*, and so forth. Different composers will invariably see or hear a scene in different ways."

It's a strict discipline whose limits to what you can and can't do can bring you down, but characteristically Quincy sees it also gives you opportunities to take chances you can't find elsewhere. "I tried everything, from twelve-tone horn parts with voices to jazz things with [bassist] Ray Brown, traditional grandiose Hollywood stuff too, the kind of music I always had fantasies about writing as a kid. All of 'em were fun trips, man. I've been so lucky. I really believe that probably the freest medium for a composer is in film scoring."

For example, "There was a sequence in *In Cold Blood*; it was a murder scene. I had a French horn, celli and low basses, three parts, very dissonant chords at the bottom, and a kind of *ostinato* underneath. Then I found this really old organ ... and I put that on top. Richard Brooks is a very mysterious director—he won't let anybody see footage of his films before they're finished—so the musicians didn't know which part they were working on. But some of us had read the book. When I put that organ part on top of this strange low bass track, our harp player got hysterical and ran out of the studio. She knew it was a murder scene. It was too heavy."

QUINCY JONES

Taking on so many scores set a breakneck pace that wreaked some havoc on Quincy's mental and physical health, but he doesn't regret taking the ball and running with it. "The music that's right for some of those situations you could never in a million years get away with putting in a record. You couldn't do it. Number one, the scene is predetermined. Sprockets are locked up until they do the final edit.

"I've always loved what that was all about ... always loved it. In the '60s, I totally immersed myself in it. I must've done 34, 35 movies in eight years. Sometimes I did eight movies a year. I just loved it. Because I waited so long to do it! To this day, Sidney Lumet and Richard Brooks call me before they do casting, which is a rare honor."

It also had an unexpected side benefit when Sidney Lumet strong-armed Quincy into paying back an old favor. In the mid-1960s, Lumet had given Quincy his first big break into movie scoring with *The Pawnbroker*. More than a decade and three films later, Sidney wanted Quincy to score another movie that wasn't exactly his cup of tea. "While I'm complaining and trying to get out of *The Wiz*, he hit me with the right words," Quincy reflects with amusement. "He said, 'You owe me.' I said, 'You're right; you got me,' and I definitely did." True to his intuition, Quincy gave *The Wiz* all he had—but it was on the film's set that he got to become reacquainted with a young performer named Michael Jackson. If he hadn't paid back that old favor, *Off the Wall*, *Thriller*, and *Bad* might have never happened.

Q with another one of his idols, Gordon Parks, on the set of *The Color Purple*, for which he was the set photographer, and a very overqualified one at that.

For two years, I shut myself off from everything to work on the movie. I sat in front of a blank screen, day after day, imagining what the film should look like. ~ Q

the most important things in my life, The Color Purple," he remembers now. "And in the middle of that, [CBS Records executive] Walter Yetnikoff said, 'You have to go out to Chicago and testify for Michael [Jackson] in a plagiarism case.' I couldn't sleep, and about quarter after nine, I turned on the TV set, and saw [the local talk show] AM Chicago. I saw this lady, and my soul jumped on fire. I said, 'She can act! She is Sofia. There's no doubt about it.' I didn't know her name; they didn't mention her name.

"I went through some of my friends and found out who she was; it was Oprah. And she was going to be the wife of Harpo. I never heard of anyone called Oprah and guess what—Oprah backwards spells 'Harpo.' And I knew it was not only my decision, it was beyond me.

"I sent a video back to Spielberg and Alice Walker. I have a video of Oprah, Whoopi, Danny Glover, and Willard Pugh doing their screen tests. He, with his usual God-given vision, gave them two lines apiece, and they had to improvise for forty minutes. That's the day they all got hired."

With everything he did behind the scenes to ensure The Color Purple's success, people sometimes forget that Quincy also made a key contribution with the score for the picture. In fact, Quincy almost forgot to do it himself, as "I had so much to do that I almost completely forgot that we needed some music. Then I suddenly realized we needed to do an hour-and-54-minute score—in eight weeks—with an entire army of gifted orchestrators and arrangers. By the time we got down to 'Miss Celie's Blues,' which was a really strong dramatic moment, [Quincy and Jeremy Lubbock's co-composer] Rod Temperton—with whom I've been collaborating for more than twenty years—and I were running out of steam, and we had

to record something the next day. So we called up Lionel Richie, who had offered earlier to finish up the lyrics if need be. And then it just flowed. It's funny, too, because Alice Walker said she didn't believe that men had written a song like that. I was also positive that we had to get [singer] Tata Vega and [blues harmonica player] Sonny Terry on it to convey the real feel."

The Color Purple is yet another milestone that wouldn't have come out the way it did if Quincy had taken no for an answer. He'd been told in no uncertain terms that "'Every idiot in town wants Steven Spielberg. He's a $5.5 million director.' Steven said to me, if you do it for scale, so will I, and he did it for $84,000. You can't have a $14 million budget and pay a director $5.5 million. They kept saying it would only do $30 million because it was an all-black picture. It did $220 million." And as a Tony-winning Broadway musical, its status as an iconic tale of twentieth-century African-American life keeps growing. "It's a continuum," Quincy believes. "It's passed, I think, the human element. It's total divinity."

top to bottom: Whoopi Goldberg as Celie.

With Danny Glover.

Co-producer Kathleen Kennedy, Spielberg, Alice Walker, Q. Between Kathleen and Steven in the background is Paulinho Da Costa, a master Brazilian percussionist and "a major player on my dream team."

"Some love from Oprah's diary that she gave me years later, which she wrote on the set of The Color Purple, walking with Alice Walker."

opposite: L to R: unidentified, Alice Walker, Steve Spielberg, Q on location in North Carolina

Oprah's Journal
June 6, 1985

Alice and I talked about Quincy "walking in the light)
He is the light. No shadows
He brings joy—just being around
him is joyous—makes me
glad I was born. I loveliness

THE COLOR PURPLE

A lice Walker's novel The Color Purple is a cornerstone literary reflection of African-American culture, so when it was made into a film, it seemed only appropriate that Quincy become involved. Movie production might not have been nearly as big a feature on his resume as record production, but once Quincy decides to do something, it's total immersion. For two years, "I shut myself off from everything to work on the movie. I sat in front of a blank screen, day after day, imagining what the film should look like. I wanted to experience every aspect of making a film."

The fellow he chose to direct the film came as a surprise, but Quincy's always shot for the top when it comes to choosing his collaborators. The honor went to Steven Spielberg, whom he'd met when Spielberg was directing E.T., a 1982 film almost as big in the world of cinema as Thriller was in pop music. Coming at a time when Quincy's work in music and other media was getting faster and more furious, Quincy also ended up producing the storybook LP for E.T., to which Michael Jackson contributed narration and a song.

"When we were trying to make Color Purple, everyone was saying, 'He is out of his mind; the first picture he's ever been involved in in his life, and he's talking about Steven Spielberg. It doesn't work like that.' But [Steven and I] were close friends. I believed he could do anything and told him that. He says, 'Shouldn't a black director do this picture?' And I said, 'No, you should. You didn't have to go to Mars to do E.T. You didn't have any experience there.' We went up to Alice Walker's, and he was very concerned and nervous. One thing led to another." Alice later told them about a lady in San Francisco, Whoopi Goldberg, who ended up playing the lead role of Celie in the movie.

Quincy can take personal credit for the discovery of the woman who would play the important supporting role of Sofia, putting her on the road to a career that eventually found her recognized as one of the influential American celebrities bar none. "I was casting one of

left: With Alice Walker, Pulitzer Prize-winning author of *The Color Purple*.

Q with (L to R) Akosua Busia and Desreta Jackson.

right top: Q with Spielberg while filming the Jook Joint scene.

right: L to R: Akosua Busia, Gordon Parks, Oprah Winfrey, Alice Walker, Q, a friend of Alice's.

Your future's so bright it burns my eyes. ~ Q

OPRAH

"The thing about Quincy is that he completely exudes and manifests love," Oprah Winfrey has observed. "Love in his work, love in his relationships, and love in all of his experiences. And so when you are listening to music that he has either created or is orchestrating or is conducting, or you are watching a film that he was a part of the production of, or you're reading a magazine that he was the publisher of, you can feel the love. That is the essence of all of the work that he does.

"I started a special journal when I went on The Color Purple. In my entire life, I've never wanted anything more than to be in that movie and won't want anything that much any more, because I never want to have to desperately want something that badly again. He was the catalyst for that; he 'discovered' me. I wrote one day, 'I've never had this feeling before. Every time I see Quincy Jones, my whole countenance lights up. He is the light.' Being around him makes you feel like he is the light, mainly because there is not a person, not a crew member, not a janitor, not a photographer, not a person passing in the airport, that he doesn't treat as though they are the best friend in his life.

"There is no division in his heart about people what-soever, and so, no matter who you are, when you are around him you feel like you're the most special person to him. That is the first time I'd ever been around anybody like that, not to mention somebody who's famous, or has the reputation that he had.

"I don't know of anybody who has the kind of drive, passion, and love for the work that he does. I've never quite experienced anybody for whom whatever project they're under-taking, that there is 100 percent of the essence of him in it, no matter what the project is."

top: With Oprah at the People's Choice Awards.

right: Oprah's date at a white-tie state White House dinner honoring the Emperor of Japan.

opposite: Oprah at the 1995 Oscars, when Q won the Jean Hersholt Humanitarian Award.

WILL SMITH

Fresh Prince of Bel-Air *was based on the life of Benny Medina, and it was in Quincy's home that the idea of having him taken in by a black family (rather than that of the real-life Jack Elliot, a white composer) was first conceived, as well as where Will Smith was cast after he read dialogue for fifteen minutes in front of twenty NBC executives who were nervous about hiring a rapper. "Will is one of the smartest and most centered young people I've met," praises Quincy. "The first day of shooting, Will didn't know where the camera was—but he learned fast and grew like a weed. The success of* Fresh Prince *in the mainstream is further proof that hip-hop has become the rock'n'roll of our era."*

It takes a lot of talent to get as far as Quincy has; it also takes a lot of talent to see those same qualities in others. Asked about his gift for detecting acting talent in performers like Smith and Oprah Winfrey, whom no one had thought to cast in a major film or television production, Quincy simply responds, "God gave me that, along with music. I don't know how it happened. I can't even drive a car, but God gave me the vision to see talent before everybody else sees it."

TELEVISION

WHEN YOU FIRST move to Hollywood to set up shop, the phone doesn't immediately ring off the hook. You've got to make some compromises, not just to get ahead in the business but to keep putting food on the table. And since it took a while for Quincy to become one of the most in-demand film scorers in the business, he got some work writing music and themes for television to pick up the slack. Though in some ways TV puts more rules on what you can and can't get away with than movies do, typically he found ways to squeeze in some innovations. A theme for *Ironside* might have been the first use of the synthesizer in a television score, and on *The Bill Cosby Show*—whose theme he co-wrote with Cosby himself—he managed to sneak in passages by top jazzmen like Cannonball Adderley, Jimmy Smith, Eddie Harris, McCoy Tyner, Milt Jackson, Oscar Peterson, Ray Brown, and Roland Kirk. He relished the opportunity to work with great jazz soloists, who could improvise to the punches and streamers (visual cues).

"I'm enjoying this so much—the opportunity to bring in these jazz soloists—that I just let them stretch out and then I cut it down later to fit my needs," he revealed in 1969. "You know how Cos is when it comes to jazz. He gets so excited and so wrapped in the recording of the scores that I can't keep him out of the studio. He's a ball to work with."

Far from being something you can coast on when you have as much talent as Quincy, television scoring turned out in some ways to be as demanding as anything he did, and he might have burned himself out fast if not for some sage advice from a couple of his mentors. When he first began scoring *Ironside* "for a 44-piece orchestra, I'd fill my score paper with sixteenth and thirty-second notes, whatever came to mind. Henry Mancini and/or Benny Carter would sometimes drop by and look over my scores and say, 'Are you crazy? You're writing 44 minutes of music weekly, like it's for a feature film.

L to R: Warren Littlefield, Benny Medina, DJ Jazzy Jeff, Jesse Jackson, Will Smith, Q, Brandon Tartikoff on the set of *The Fresh Prince*.

In the House

MAD tv

This is TV, Q, use whole notes, long sustained passages with your strings and horns. Let a solo instrument, your rhythm section, or our bass player do the dancing on top. Don't try to write Stravinsky's 'Firebird Suite' for every episode, or you'll never live through the year.' I finally got the message, but it was still a crushing workload."

Quincy's compositions for Episode 1 of *Roots*, one of the three most watched programs in the history of television, won him an Emmy in 1977.

With a pilot directed by Debbie Allen, his production company got the hit show *Fresh Prince of Bel-Air* on the air, starring young rapper Will Smith, as well as the comedy series *MADtv* and *In the House*. There was even some time to fit in some guest appearances on *Fresh Prince* and *Ironside*, and guest host a 1990 episode of *Saturday Night Live* that was shot and aired the very night of Nelson Mandela's release from a South African prison.

Quincy's no snob and knows that advancement for African Americans

has to take place on all fronts, whether through serious sociopolitical agendas or popular culture. Television's one place you can send the message to hundreds of millions of people of all kinds, and several of his TV projects have done a lot to give African Americans their due on television, the biggest mass media form of our age. "In the '30s and early '40s, we had no role models," he reminds us. "How can anybody grow up and aspire to something if it doesn't exist?" By producing *Fresh Prince of Bel-Air*, Quincy was able to take matters into his own hands after growing "tired of knocking on doors and asking, 'Do you think this is a good idea?' or 'Would you like to do this?' At this stage in my life and career, I don't have time to convince somebody else that something might work. The black experience is a funny experience. It's very rich. It's colorful. It's the juice of American pop culture."

top left: On *Saturday Night Live* in 1990, with Mike Myers, Q was the host and musical guest.

top right: With Will Smith.

Q's company QDE produced the shows *MADtv* and *In The House*.

How do you know "this person is it, this person is gonna work" versus somebody else? How did he know that Will Smith was *The Fresh Prince of Bel-Air*? I don't know how he does that. That's his gift. He just operates from the purest place. He will tell you that he always leaves room for God to walk in the door, whether he's creating music, whether he's creating a television show, a television special, whether he's producing the Oscars, whatever he's doing. He recognizes that there is a larger connection with him, his music, his work, his art. He knows that, and I think all the true artists do. You know that what you do you don't do alone. ~ OPRAH

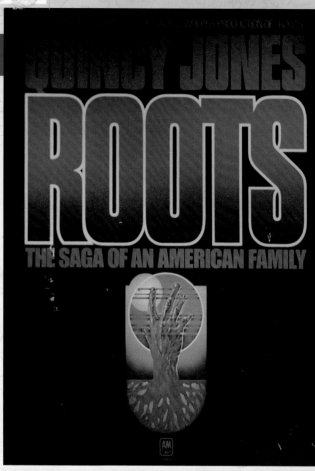

As much as he's done to expand American jazz and pop into new directions, Quincy's always been interested in tracing the roots of African-American music back to Africa itself. Roots was the project that gave him his biggest canvas for painting that journey with sound, recorded in the twentieth century but dipping into a well several centuries deep.

Quincy first met author Alex Haley around the beginning of the 1960s, but it would not be until 1977 that they had the chance to combine forces when Haley's Roots was made into an epochal TV miniseries, following the journey of a black family from Africa through slavery and the Civil Rights era. When Haley ran out of funds while researching the book, Quincy and his wife, actress Peggy Lipton, even lent him money so he could complete the project. As Peggy remembered, "His researcher, George Sims, and Alex spent a lot of time with us, and every new discovery they made was like we were part of it."

As Quincy had talked up his hopes to do projects road-mapping the evolution of black American music from its African origins to the late twentieth century to the press on several occasions, it was only natural that he be tapped to write the score. In Lipton's words, "Quincy was very much involved in Alex's process with Roots. It touched him so deeply, the subject matter, that he felt he had to be involved, and he did a tremendous amount of research. For many, many nights, he'd be in his studio when I could hear African voices, African rhythms. He met with Letta Mbulu, he worked with her, and he had all the finest African musicians. But he really went into the research, too, because he wanted it just right."

Unfortunately, he was replaced after just one episode, though he did get to put together the Roots LP of music used in and inspired by the program, which came out shortly after the series was broadcast. "I got dismissed from Roots after the first episode because the first episode was about the homeland," he explains. "I said, 'If they're going to take this music away after this episode, then this episode is very important to have what the essence of African music was about.' They said, 'We don't give a

shit about this. This is for the Middle West. We couldn't care less about that. It's not going fast enough, you know.'"

The huge success of the series was so unexpected that Quincy had to cut short a vacation in Seattle to produce the Roots LP—"the fastest I've ever done anything in my life," he notes. "I had to put that record together with the translations of all the African words and all that stuff. I think we sold 500,000 copies in less than 24 hours."

But the music Quincy wrote for Roots had a message that couldn't be measured by sales, as impressive as they were. In his view, "African music had always been regarded in the West as primitive and savage, but when you take the time to really study it, you see that it's as structured and sophisticated as European classical music, with the same basic components as you'll find in a symphony orchestra—instruments that are plucked, instruments that are beaten, and instruments that are blown with reeds. And it's music from the soul—powerful, elemental... From gospel, blues, jazz, soul, R&B, rock'n'roll, all the way to rap, you can trace the roots straight back to Africa."

WE ARE THE WORLD

CHECK YOUR LOONEY-TUDES AT THE DOOR!

DEAR QUINCY

Q, NOW A STAR IN EVERY DIMENSION !!! LOVE R

WITH LOVE, Chuck Jones

top: Check your Looney Tunes at the door! A salute to "We Are the World."

above: The Christmas episode of *Boondocks*.

right: This sketch was drawn for Q by his dear friend Chuck Jones the day after Q's brother Lloyd died.

opposite: Q, George Benson, Alex Haley, and Sidney Poitier hangin' at Q's house.

4

MENTORING A
BETTER WORLD

Imagine what a harmonious world it could be
if every single person, both young and old,
shared a little of what he is good at doing. ~ Q

MENTORING A BETTER WORLD

TO MAKE YOUR WAY in a business where far more people fail than succeed, you need a lot of help from older and wiser men and women who can show you how it's done and give you the break or two you need. Now that he's one of those wiser, more experienced men himself, Quincy Jones is as eager as ever to give kudos to the many mentors crucial to his coming of age as both a musician and a man. Starting with the big-band heroes of his youth, the roll call would also include trumpeter Clark Terry, composition teacher Nadia Boulanger, record executive Irving Green, film director Sidney Lumet, and trusted friends and business associates Time Warner CEO Steve Ross and music executive Clarence Avant.

As Quincy himself became a music legend and man of the world, it was only natural that he in turn would become an inspiration to others in the entertainment business, from newcomers all the way up to superstars Michael Jackson, Oprah Winfrey, and Will Smith. He's taken such leadership another step forward in the last few dec-ades, however, by expanding his reach beyond the world of show business. The field he's now operating in is bigger than any musical stage, bigger even than those record-breaking sales figures for *Thriller*. These days he's dedicating his energy and creativity to humanitarian projects more massive in scale than almost any others attempted by fellow celebrities of his stature.

"Somebody told me when I was very young that there are three phases you go through," he explains today. "That's the quest for materialism, which is survival, especially if you're going to [be in] Chicago. Then, psychologically, a quest for power, to see if money means anything. That's all normal and that's natural, which you're supposed to go through, before you give and don't expect anything in return. That to me is the best feeling in the world, when you see kids that didn't have a chance, where you could do a little bit to help or involve an organization that could help."

Mentorship, he reflects, "is a strange thing. You're not really aware that's what you're doing. Albert Schweitzer

previous page: Q in South Africa with Nelson Mandela during the "South Central to South Africa" trip.

opposite: Mandela during the "Democracy Now" trip. "Arthur Ashe sat next to me on the plane, and together we conceived of a 'music and sports Olympics.' He's one of my all-time heroes."

With a group of talented South African musicians at a reception held by the U.S. Ambassador to South Africa.

said, 'It's done by example, by example, by example.' They don't listen to what you say; they listen to what you do. I learn by having a lot of kids and having a lot of mentors; I watch what *they* do. That's what's really important—do they walk the talk." Part of that is urging up-and-comers not to think small. "The young kids always ask me what I recommend," he muses. "I say, 'Want more! Dream more! Don't get hung up on this little jive lame dream down here. Get a big one out there. And then if you get halfway there, you're still okay. But make it big.'"

Quincy's production of the 1985 "We Are the World" single, which boosted global awareness of the need to aid Ethiopian famine victims and raised more than $63 million for the cause, was his first philanthropic endeavor to attract widespread attention. There are very few people alive who weren't touched in some way by what was much more than just a #1 record. By bringing attention to an urgent cause, he helped make uncounted millions aware that something needed to be done. That even goes for millions of people who never bought the record nor heard it on the radio.

But Quincy's social activism, like that of so many African Americans of his generation, far predated the mid-1980s. It's no passing fancy or bandwagon to hitch

a ride with; it can be traced back to the beginnings of the Civil Rights Movement. He'd been an activist by example within the music industry, of course, becoming the first black executive at a major white-owned record company, and the first major black film composer in Hollywood. Yet he'd also crossed paths with Martin Luther King, Jr., starting in the mid-1950s, and by the early 1970s was working with young emerging political leader Jesse Jackson on projects benefiting the African-American community.

After "We Are the World," Quincy's initiatives became more ambitious and larger in scope. His Quincy Jones Foundation has collaborated with Nelson Mandela to build homes in South Africa. He's one of the founders and guiding forces behind We Are the Future, an initiative devoted to bettering the lives of underprivileged children throughout the world, launched by a 2004 concert in Rome before half a million people. With the Harvard School of Public Health, he's created the Q Prize to honor international leadership in advocates of child welfare. He's also found time to lend his support to numerous other charities, including the NAACP, the Gay & Lesbian Alliance Against Defamation, Peace Games (geared toward educating children to become peacemakers), and amfAR (the Foundation for AIDS Research).

It's quite a list, and a big part of a lifetime journey that's taken Quincy from the Chicago ghetto to being an honored guest of the world's top leaders, from President Bill Clinton, whose 1993 inauguration gala he produced, to Pope John Paul II. But Quincy's never forgotten where he came from. Through it all, he's also kept strong mentorship ties with the African-American music community, promoting social responsibility among rappers and hip-hoppers, and continuing to champion music in general as the best way to bring people together. "I think there is nothing in the world, probably since the beginning of time, that connects people in a stronger way than music does," he declares. "It's the only absolute outside of mathematics. It's the only thing that engages the left and the right brain simultaneously, the emotional and the intellect. That's why they are using it to cure Down syndrome and autism; it's powerful stuff. You can't see it, you can't taste it, you can't smell it, you can't touch it, but you can sure feel it."

In all his work, whether artistic or humanitarian or a combination of the two, Quincy continues to emphasize the importance of transcending racial and cultural borders. If you love the music of another race and country, you're going to be a lot more inclined to get along. "Somehow everybody learns how to

communicate with the other person with respecting their culture, and not trying to enforce their [own] culture on other people," he feels. "That bothers me more than anything else—'I don't agree with you, you're going to do it my way, and if I don't agree with you, I'm going to kill you.' I don't know where that comes from. It's got to be a man thing, because women give life, and I don't think they think like that. We have to just hope that other people care enough to do something that can divert that violence."

Putting people in contact is a key to Quincy's hopes for a better and more peaceful world. "It's about stereotypes and preconceived ideas," he feels. "People that don't get around each other never get to know each other. My remedy for trying to cure some of the things is just getting people together so they can notice this and say, 'Hey, he's not a bad guy.'"

In keeping with that philosophy, educating youth is the focus of Quincy's concerns these days more than anything else. "Education is number one," he proclaims. "The amount of money that the French can spend on ice-cream in four months could educate every child in the world. What the girls from fourteen to eighteen years [old] in America spend on cosmetics could educate every child in the world."

Every kid deserves a start, no matter where they come from. The reality is that two-thirds of the kids in the world are going through this. ~ Q

clockwise from top left: At the Children's School and Hospital in Angkor Wat in Cambodia. "Check out sweet little Jojo in the lower left, wearing the red sweater!"

During a tour of South Africa, visiting a transition home for babies orphaned or abandoned as a result of AIDS.

On the "South Central to South Africa" trip.

opposite clockwise from top left: Relaxing with Nelson Mandela at Mandela's home in 2006.

Q in Rwanda during the anniversary of the genocide. Q was invited by his close friend President Paul Kagame.

With Ms. Shabazz, Malcolm X's daughter, on the "South Central to South Africa" trip.

Speaking at the U.N.

EARLY SOCIAL ACTIVISM

WHEN QUINCY FIRST MET the man who did more than anyone to spark the Civil Rights Movement, the Civil Rights Act was about a decade away. Segregation had just been outlawed in public schools, but it was still the law of much of the land in many facets of public life, especially in the South. "I met Martin Luther King in 1955 at a daytime concert I had with my band," he remembers. "I was broke as the Ten Commandments, and we played the benefit at Jackie Robinson's house in Connecticut. Everybody was there. This man had a coat over his arm and a white shirt with sleeves rolled up, and we both had a beer. He said, 'My name is Martin King.' I worked with him all over the country like everybody else did, concerts and Carnegie Hall and all that. Every movement of black activism has been preceded by a new black music, and this was when modern jazz had just begun."

Growing up in Chicago and Seattle, Jones hadn't been exposed to the worst excesses of American racism. When you're in a big band like Lionel Hampton's, however, you've got to put the South on your tour schedule, and the hatred suffered by your brothers and sisters down there smack you in the face. At the time, "Hamp would do 70 straight one-nighters in the Carolinas. And we'd go through these little towns, and you know you were in ... almost like in *enemy* territory. There's an attitude that you could just *smell*. You could almost just *taste* it, you know. With the hate stares, and everything else. It just ... it just had a *smell* to it."

So Quincy had never been blind to racial injustice, but the assassination of King in April 1968 was a profound shock that lit a match under his urges to get involved in social activism. "I had never been that political before, but following the mule-drawn wagon carrying Dr. King's casket through the streets of Memphis in a crowd of thousands pushed me right to the edge," he wrote in his autobiography. "I had gone down to the funeral with Marlon Brando, Haskell Wexler, James Baldwin, Norman Jewison, Tony Franciosa, Hal Ashby, and Cesar Chavez. We all slept on a hotel floor down there and were enormously affected by the whole experience."

Not long afterward his friend, bandleader and singer Billy Eckstine, introduced Quincy to a young dynamic African American named Jesse Jackson. Long before becoming a household name and presidential candidate, Jackson had been vital to King's establishment of the Southern Christian Leadership Conference in Chicago, becoming the SCLC's national director in 1967. In the early 1970s, Quincy went back to his hometown to volunteer to serve on the board of Jackson's Operation PUSH (People United to Save Humanity), helping the organization champion social and economic justice for African Americans. "In 1968, after Dr. King was assassinated and there was a great furor and a great tension, Quincy came back to Chicago and sought me out," recalled Jackson. "He felt a need to address himself to the agony of that period."

The two remained tight, and about twenty years later Quincy became convinced that Jesse needed to address himself to the whole nation on a regular basis. But though the eponymous television talk show that Quincy created for him in 1990 didn't last long, Jones's admiration for the politician remained high. (Jackson's subsequent CNN talk show lasted for eight years.) As Quincy put it, "He cares about the common man, the man or woman who doesn't have a voice on TV, from coal miners in Virginia to farmers in Iowa. He understands that. He feels that."

INSTITUTE FOR BLACK AMERICAN MUSIC

WHEN HE WAS ON the board of Operation PUSH in the early 1970s, Quincy got one of his first chances to combine what's proven to be his biggest passions, music and social activism. With several other board members—including chairman Jerry Butler, Roberta Flack, Cannonball Adderley, Nat Adderley, Donny Hathaway, and Isaac Hayes—Quincy founded the Institute for Black American Music in the early 1970s. They didn't just take its mission into the classroom, holding seminars for local high schools; in the best tradition of putting your lessons into practice, he and his fellow Institute members also put on a show. Not any old show, but seven star-studded nights at the Chicago Amphitheater with Stevie Wonder, the Supremes, the Jackson Five, and Marvin Gaye; comedians Flip Wilson, Richard Pryor, Dick Gregory, and Bill Cosby; and even the cast of *Sesame Street*. The 1973 Duke Ellington special on CBS television that Quincy co-produced (and for which he conducted the orchestra) was also a project of the Institute, and Jones also co-founded the Black Arts Festival in Chicago.

Quincy's role in the Institute is just one more example of his longtime commitment to honoring the importance of African American musical heritage and passing it on to new generations. If you don't keep your tradition alive, it's in danger of dying, whether passed on by speech, song, and deed back in historical Africa, or by classes, performances, or records in our modern age. "I would like more young people to see the whole thread, rather than get split up, because you see it's too costly to put a crown on James Brown's head, while his feet are in the blood of Duke Ellington," he said at the time. "It can't be cut off like that, and it hurts me to see it. It shouldn't be the ego trip of who I am, but it should be, look who we are."

Along the same lines, he added a few years later, "The musicologists tried to deal with African music and its extensions in terms of the European art forms, whereas the African forms had nothing to do with that. African life was a total life force harnessed to the music. We didn't have writers, but we did have the music, and the music was the vehicle to carry the remnants of black history. The *true* history of blacks is not in our history books, but in the music. The only blacks I ever heard of in school were Booker T. Washington and George Washington Carver. It was like nobody else existed. We had no folk heroes in any books, ever. Our history is all locked in the music and is passed down in its different forms through that music."

opposite: L to R: Ed Bradley, The Good Doctor, Lionel Hampton, Peggy Lipton-Jones at a T. J. Martell Cancer Foundation event.

Receiving the Marian Anderson Award from Mayor Street at a church ceremony in Philadelphia in 2001.

WE ARE THE WORLD

Aside from Thriller, the 1985 "We Are the World" single is probably the most famous recording that Quincy Jones has produced, and not solely for musical reasons. Yes, it did make #1 in the U.S. and several other countries, sell more than five million copies in the U.S. alone, and bring together dozens of superstars for the recording session. But for Quincy, these weren't the most important things it did. No, its most important achievement was generating aid for one of the most impoverished regions of the planet.

Quincy had a big part to play in "We Are the World," but makes it clear that it grew out of the concern and efforts of a large number of people. The idea kicked off when Harry Belafonte thought that something should be done about the hundreds of thousands of Ethiopians starving as famine and civil war raged in their country. Promoter Ken Kragen and singer Lionel Richie, says Quincy, "called me after Belafonte called them to tell them that Live Aid was doing this, and we were doing nothing. They had heard a record I did called 'State of Independence' with Donna [Summer]. There were sixteen bars, and I said to myself, 'This should be a choir, and I want the best forces in the world.' So I had a third of the people of 'We Are the World' sing on that sixteen-bar phrase, and I'm sure that that's how it all started."

At first, Quincy continues, Belafonte was talking about doing a tour with numerous star musicians, but "you could never get that group to go on the road. So we took it up to 46 people and did it" in the studio. All those people did indeed participate in the recording session for the "We Are the World" single on January 28, 1985; the twenty-one singers sharing the lead vocals included Lionel Richie, Michael Jackson, Stevie Wonder, Paul Simon, Tina Turner, Billy Joel, Diana Ross, Dionne Warwick, Willie Nelson, Bruce Springsteen, Bob Dylan, and Ray Charles. Even the behind-the-scenes staff, such as sound engineer Humberto Gatica and vocal arranger Tom Bahler, were superstars in their fields.

A Doonesbury Book by GB Trudeau.

Check Your Egos at the Door

It was Quincy's suggestion to have Lionel Richie and Michael Jackson write the song, and Quincy who urged the pair to complete the tune after he found it hadn't yet been composed when he called them shortly before the session. "In those days Michael would like nothing better than to sit around and write, so those two took it on," is how Quincy's remembered the collaboration taking shape. "Two weeks before the session, I started calling Michael's house to listen to what they came up with, and sure enough he and Lionel were there hangin', sitting around talking about Motown and old times. I said, 'My dear brothers, we have 46 stars coming in less than three weeks, and we need a damn song.' Lionel came up with something first. He played a cassette with the melody on the title lines for Michael. Michael locked himself in his house for a couple of days and finished the rest. The lyrics were written by the two of them."

It was by no means a given that the cream of the pop star elite would show up when the session came around. "We didn't have that many people at first," says Quincy of the all-star cast assembled to record the song. "These people came in to do something and try to help the people in Ethiopia, they really cared; they came in with their hearts wide open to do this right. We didn't know what was going to happen."

You could have forgiven Quincy for being afraid all these stars in one place might try to elbow each other out of the picture, whether from the video being filmed or the vocal parts that had to be shared among dozens of men and women used to having the spotlight all to themselves. But he'd already thought of that, posting a friendly warning in the letter that he sent out to all the artists asking them to participate: "Check your egos at the door." The slogan actually originated—by Chicago soul great Jerry Butler, Quincy thinks—back when Jones helped create the Institute for Black American Music in Chicago in the early 1970s.

We Are The World

Written by Michael Jackson and Lionel Richie

There comes a time when we heed a certain call
When the world must come together as one
There are people dying
And it's time to lend a hand to life
The greatest gift of all

We can't go on pretending day by day
That someone, somewhere will soon make a change
We are all a part of God's great big family
And the truth, you know,
Love is all we need

CHORUS:
We are the world, we are the children
We are the ones who make a brighter day
So let's start giving
There's a choice we're making
We're saving our own lives
It's true we'll make a better day
Just you and me

Send them your heart so they'll know that someone cares
And their lives will be stronger and free
As God has shown us by turning stones to bread
So we all must lend a helping hand

REPEAT CHORUS:

When you're down and out, there seems no hope at all
But if you just believe there's no way we can fall
Let us realize that a change can only come
When we stand together as one

REPEAT CHORUS

© 1985 Mijac Music (BMI) and Brockman Music (ASCAP)
All rights on behalf of Mijac Music (BMI) adm. by Warner — Tamerlane Publishing Corp.
All rights reserved. Used by permission.

B/W "GRACE"
By Quincy Jones and Jeremy Lubbock
© 1984 Quincy Jones d/b/a/ YellowBrick Road Music (ASCAP) and
Neropub/Hollysongs (BMI) adm. by Shankman/DeBlasio.

Associate Producer: Tom Bahler. Engineered by Humberto Gatica and John Guess.
Mastered by Stephen Marcussen at Precision Lacquer. Art Direction: John Coulter.
Photography: Sam Emerson and Henry Diltz.
Cover art by John Lykes with special thanks to Roland Young.

USA for AFRICA
United Support of Artists for Africa

United Support of Artists for Africa ("USA for AFRICA") is a non-profit corporation formed to help the millions of suffering people in Africa and the United States. All profits realized by CBS Records from the sale of "We Are The World" will be contributed to USA for AFRICA. USA for AFRICA has pledged to use these funds to address immediate emergency needs in the USA and Africa, including food and medicine, and to help the African people become self-sufficient. By buying this record, you are playing an important part in the fight to end an ongoing tragedy that affects *all* of us—because "We Are The World."

If you wish to contribute directly to USA for AFRICA, your donation may be sent to: USA for AFRICA, c/o Jess S. Morgan & Company, Accountants, 6420 Wilshire Blvd., Ste. 1900, Los Angeles, CA 90048

Columbia
Jeffrey Osborne appears courtesy of A & M Records, Inc.; Dionne Warwick appears courtesy of Arista Records; Bette Midler appears courtesy of Atlantic Recording Corp.; Michael Boddicker appears courtesy of Boddifications; Tina Turner and Louis Johnson appear courtesy of Capitol Records; Bob Geldof appears courtesy of CBS Records/PolyGram Records Ltd.; Huey Lewis & The News appear courtesy of Chrysalis Records; Bod Dylan, Billy Joel, Kenny Loggins, Willie Nelson, Steve Perry and Bruce Springsteen appear courtesy of Columbia Records; Lindsey Buckingham appears courtesy of Elektra/Asylum Records; Kim Carnes appears courtesy of EMI-America Records; Jackie Jackson, Marlon Jackson, Michael Jackson, Randy Jackson and Tito Jackson appear courtesy of Epic Records; Lionel Richie, Smokey Robinson and Stevie Wonder appear courtesy of Motown Record Corporation; Paulinho da Costa appears courtesy of Pablo Records; The Pointer Sisters and Greg Phillinganes appear courtesy of Planet Records; Cyndi Lauper appears courtesy of Portrait Records; LaToya Jackson appears courtesy of Private I Records; James Ingram and Quincy Jones appear courtesy of Qwest Records; Hall & Oates, Waylon Jennings, Kenny Rogers and Diana Ross appear courtesy of RCA Records; Michael Omartian appears courtesy of Sparrow Records; Al Jarreau, John Robinson, Sheila E. and Paul Simon appear courtesy of Warner Bros. Records Inc.

Quincy had also used an imaginary sign with those same words for Michael Jackson's Off the Wall sessions.

But ultimately it proved "totally unnecessary because everybody came ready to really give it up. Everyone, that is, except Cindy Lauper's manager, who said, 'We got a problem, man. The rockers don't like the song.'" Yet when it was discussed with "rockers" Billy Joel, Bruce Springsteen, Steve Perry, Hall & Oates, and Lauper herself, "They all claimed to love the song."

That wasn't the only problem Quincy had to contend with in simply getting a session of such size to come off. In preparation, "We really had it laid out. Where they stand, who was going to sing the solos—only 21 out of 46—which was already getting dangerous. And sure enough, when we were doing the last parts, the line was 'We are the world,' and Michael had written a little fill that went 'sha la, sha lingay.' Well, [Bob] Geldof stopped everything and said, 'Oh, no, we can't do that. The Africans will think we're making fun of them.' And I said, 'Here it is. Turn off the cameras. However it works out, won't matter.'

"Pretty soon they started taking sides, volunteering opinions. And then Stevie [Wonder] decides to call somebody in Ghana to get the right pronunciation in Swahili. Around three o'clock in the morning, he comes wandering back in with it taped on his ghetto blaster and says, 'Can I have

your attention, please. The correct words for this thing should be willy moingu.' Well, that was too much for Ray Charles. He said, 'Man, it's three o'clock in the goddamned morning, and I can't even sing in English, man. Screw Willy and Moingu, too!' Man, what a night that was!"

Eventually all the kinks got worked out, and the "We Are the World" single, when combined with the album and video also featuring the song, raised more than $60 million for the cause that had sparked its creation. The producer also notes that the project "reportedly prodded the U.S. government to spend $800 million more in the same cause." Adds Quincy, "I have never before or since experienced the joy I felt that night working with this rich, complex human tapestry of love, talent, and grace ... Overall it was one of the most successful and unified outreaches ever in the music world."

We had a lots of puzzles to solve... like textures of voices that had to go with each other... and totally diverse backgrounds, from country & western to middle-of-the-road to legends... There's one standard in music that transcends all the styles, and that's a quality and a willingness to become a whole... Having that many people in the room that night—if they hadn't wanted to come together, it wouldn't have turned out the same way... Everything worked... God was never with us more on any project than that night. ~ Q

top left to right: During the recording session. Stevie Wonder, Michael Jackson, Lionel Richie.
opposite top left to right: Bruce Springsteen and Q. Smokey Robinson, Q, Lionel Richie, and Michael Jackson.

With Desmond Tutu at a Nelson Mandela's Children's Fund event.

opposite top: The "South Central to South Africa" delegation, with Nelson Mandela and his daughter Zinzi.

THE QUINCY JONES FOUNDATION

QUINCY JONES KNOWS that young people aren't only at risk in the inner cities of the United States: It's a global problem, not one confined to any one nation or any type of neighborhood. It's also a problem that governments haven't been able to solve, and one he takes seriously enough to have started the Quincy Jones Listen Up Foundation (now simply the Quincy Jones Foundation) in 1991 to "confront the state of emergency that currently threatens the world's youth." Its projects have ranged from "From South Central to South Africa," which sent five Los Angeles youths to build homes in South Africa, to developing a curriculum about black music in America for more than 100,000 classrooms. And it's not just about reaching out to gangs and students, but also about starting a "Q Fellowship Program" for, in Quincy's words, giving "a future generation of African entrepreneurs and social innovators vital exposure to the private, public, and non-profit sectors that are at the forefront of the rapidly changing techno-

logical landscape. The 'Q Fellows' will in turn be able to apply that knowledge and use technology in their communities to develop lasting economic viability."

The Foundation has been especially active in South Africa, and its work there has enhanced the strong friendship between Quincy and Nelson Mandela, the great anti-apartheid leader and former president of the nation. "With Nelson Mandela, we go to his home for dinner, we visit the children with HIV and see them in debates about abstinence versus condoms and all that stuff," he says. "South Africa has been through it now. Last year they had 25,000 murders, 60 percent were women, and that's a country of 40 million people. I've seen what they've accomplished in those roughest times—you can't even imagine." As for Mandela himself, as Quincy notes in admiration, "I don't know what it takes to go through what he went through and not be angry, and violent, and destructive or resentful ... Maybe he's found the power of converting darkness into light."

SOUTH CENTRAL TO SOUTH AFRICA

One of the Foundation's most celebrated projects was one in which Quincy himself got to participate. "I had promised Mandela that we would build 100 homes."

So in 2001, Quincy "decided to take five gang-bangers from South Central [Los Angeles]. And in ten days, 10,000 miles from home, they understood the spirit of Ubuntu, which means that the collective is always more important than the individual. To see this woman who had lived in a cardboard box with no water, electricity, all these years walk into her own home with a stove, electric lights and everything else— it doesn't get any better than that."

These tough, seen-it-all kids from South Central got down on their knees and cried like babies when they met Nelson Mandela. And the payoff didn't end when the kids went back to LA, as "the kids now, they're all in executive positions with organizations helping kids get out of trouble."

I don't think it should surprise anybody that a guy with Quincy's level of energy and imagination would want to be acquainted with people not just in the music world, but also in politics and in other areas of life as well. When he decided that he wanted to be more of a citizen with more impact to go beyond civil rights into other issues as well, things that were outside his own direct experience—one thing I've always been impressed with is he goes after that the same way he went after music. Quincy never gets tired of learning, and I think that's a great part of his genius and a great reason for his impact.

~ PRESIDENT BILL CLINTON

With Naomi Campbell and Nelson Mandela on a Foundation trip that also included Chip Lyons, Chris Stamos, Kim Samuel-Johnson, and Graca Machel.

VIBE MAGAZINE HIP-HOP SYMPOSIUM

clockwise from top: Suge Knight and Dr. Dre.

L to R: Public Enemy, Chuck D, Ernie Singleton, John Singleton.

P. Diddy.

opposite top left: John Singleton.

top center: Fab 5 Freddy with Colin Powell.

Just as Quincy made the transition from jazz to soul, funk, and pop, so has he been at ease collaborating with the hip-hop generation—and not just musically, though he's done that as well on albums like 1990's Back on the Block. He's also been a mentor and role model for rappers on both musical and personal grounds, earning thumbs-ups from the likes of Melle Mel and Wyclef Jean. Ludacris sampled Quincy's "Soul Bossa Nova" on his 2005 single "Number One Spot," Jones even appearing in the video; Tupac sampled "Body Heat" for his biggest hit, "How Do U Want It"; and Kanye West sampled "P.Y.T." for his recent single "Good Life." Quincy is releasing a brand new hip-hop album with Akon, Wyclef, Snoop Dogg, Jamie Foxx, and a host of others. In addition, Quincy and Usher teamed with Habitat for Humanity in 2007 to promote ongoing relief efforts for the victims of Hurricane Katrina, later initiating a camp targeted toward getting Gulf Coast youth to complete a service project.

Rap has been an unofficial language of sorts for youngsters all over the English-speaking world for years now. But with the world shrinking more every day as songs travel instantaneously online and by satellite, Quincy also sees the possibilities rap offers for spreading positive messages on a global level. "I personally feel that the rappers could revolutionize education

around the world," he says. "We've got the ear of every young person on the planet, and every country in the world has pushed their indigenous music aside to use our music, mainly black music, the Esperanto."

Toward that end, in 1995 Quincy hosted a symposium of leading voices in rap music at New York's Peninsula hotel to exchange musical and social ideas. "If we come up with one thing, it'll be to realize that you can not afford to any longer be nonpolitical," he urged at the time. "It's great to talk about chillin' and everything else, but there's something more important. You have too much power to not be political. You have to say something. You have to talk about something. This is about talented people. But the content is real serious; it reaches the whole world." Also in attendance was future Secretary of State Colin Powell, who joked, "The real reason I'm here is that Quincy Jones ordered me to be here. And I take orders."

Revealed Quincy afterward, "I confiscated all videotapes and film to protect Colin Powell, who wound up staying for five hours instead of two. I didn't want anyone using photos or footage to damage him if he decided to run for the presidency, which he was contemplating at the time. Some of the younger rappers didn't even know who he was. When addressing some of the more confrontational comments from

the floor, Powell maintained his South Bronx demeanor and authoritative cool throughout."

The idea of the summit, as Quincy observed a few years later, was "to get rappers in the hip-hop community to build their own coalition so they're not influenced by external forces, really. And they don't get blown away so young. It's unacceptable, and we've got to change whatever it is that's happening to cause it."

Was it a success? For Quincy and his family, there was a bitter aftermath, as "I had just begun to connect with Tupac Shakur, who was engaged to my daughter Kidada before he was gunned down in Las Vegas. Though we got off to a rocky start, as I came to know and feel him, I saw his enormous potential and sensitivity as an artist and as a human being. I'll never forget that when he made an appointment to meet me at the Bel Air Hotel, he arrived promptly at ten, then left a message with the maître d' that he'd be back in a suit and tie. He wanted to greet me respectfully, not just as an artist and entrepreneur but as the father of the woman he loved. This is the side of Tupac that the media and his fans never saw, because of the mythology of the gangsta prose."

I see a connection between hip-hop and bebop. They both had to invent their own language. You know, "If you don't let us in your culture, then we'll start our own." ~ Q

HUMANITARIAN EFFORTS

top, left to right: The *America's Millennium* concert at the Washington Monument.

Q speaking about technology at the Pacific Rim Conference with Clinton, Gore, Ron Brown, and the governor of Oregon.

Ronald and Nancy Reagan at the White House.

opposite, clockwise from top left: With Bill Clinton at the Concert of the Americas, which Q co-produced in Miami for the presidents of 34 Latin American countries.

With Hillary Clinton the morning after Q spent the night in Lincoln's bedroom at the White House, January 1, 2000, following the Millennium Concert, which Q produced with George Stevens.

L to R: Q, unidentified, Colin Powell, Superior Court Judge Richard Jones (Q's brother) at the American Academy of Achievement Awards.

THE DEEPER QUINCY got involved in international humanitarian efforts, the more he came into close contact with several of the most powerful politicians of the late twentieth century. It's one thing to share studios with Frank Sinatra and Michael Jackson; it's a whole different ballgame to be ushered into the confidences of heads of state throughout the globe. These included not just Nelson Mandela and Colin Powell, but also Archbishop Desmond Tutu and French president Jacques Chirac. Not the least of his high-powered friends is Bill Clinton, at whose 1993 inaugural celebration Quincy served as executive producer, in which film footage of Martin Luther King, Jr., was followed with a live performance by rapper LL Cool J.

"I was very pleased when Bill mentioned how he dug the correlation between Dr. King's protest of the '50s and LL Cool's protest of the '90s," says Quincy Jones in retrospect. "It's the same cloth." He's also pleased not only "that the president understood it, but that 500,000 other people did. They jumped to their feet when he hit that stage. They leaped off the ground when LL came out after Dr. King. It fit so organically, it was like a glove." Quincy later was executive producer of *An American Celebration*, a televised 2000 millennium concert, for Clinton as well.

"I think Quincy understood that if we're really going to be the first kind of modern president, it wouldn't be enough to be the first rock'n'roll president, because that was my childhood," is how Clinton himself reacted. "I had to be the first president of all those young people who were old enough to vote and were, among other things, into rap music."

As you'd guess, Quincy's also teamed up with other music-minded folks in his philanthropic efforts, and in recent years, Quincy's often worked alongside Bono, the two sharing a passion for using their music and celebrity for positive sociopolitical change. "Bono is my brother from another mother," says Quincy when recalling how the pair met. "Bono told me how he had been influenced by [British band] New Order, who was on my [Qwest] label, from Manchester. We sat and talked until daylight, just totally bonded like that, and have ever since. We go all over the world together. He brought his whole family to the Millennium [extravaganza] when I produced it, to just sing one number, the song 'One.' We are partners in crime; there's nobody like him."

We're not, any of us, above being a groupie when it comes to somebody like Quincy Jones. ~ COLIN POWELL

À Quincy Jones, en Témoignage d'estime, avec ma très cordiale admiration et mes sincères amitiés,

J. CHIRAC
26-3-2001

Jacques Chirac's kindness always overwhelmed me. No matter what event we were at at the palace, he always excused himself to walk me to my car. His wife, Bernadette, and daughter Claude were also the embodiments of graciousness. ~ Q

right: Claude Nobs, Rosemary Tomich, Muriel Robin, Henri Salvador, President Chirac, Anouk Aimee, Line Renaud, Quincy, Kenya.

FRENCH LEGION d'HONNEUR

Quincy's not only been recognized for his work at the highest levels of American government. He's also been given honors of the highest degrees overseas, as he was on March 26, 2001, when he was made a Legion d'Honneur Commander by French president Jacques Chirac. It's the highest civil honor the French government can bestow upon a man. Jones was the first American-born musician to receive it, having already been made a chevalier of the Legion in 1990.

While most of Quincy's accomplishments, musical and otherwise, have been achieved in his native United States, it was in France where Quincy had some of his most formative experiences as a young adult, studying composition with Nadia Boulanger; enjoying his first position of prominence with a record label, as musical director of Barclay Disques; and presenting some of the first performances by the big band he'd take through Europe in 1960.

DEBT RELIEF

QUINCY KEEPS A WICKED sense of humor in the unlikeliest and holiest of places, as Bono found out when the pair visited Pope John Paul II in 1999 on behalf of Third World debt relief. "We noticed these friezes on the wall," he remembered. "The apostles, they're sitting in these fantastic tapestries, and they've all got amazing hand movements. And Q's going, 'That's dope, you see that? See, that's where the brothers got it from.' And I was, 'Wow, you're exactly right!'"

When it came time for Quincy to shake the Pope's hand, he couldn't help but notice that "all the rest of the guys in the Vatican had these industrial black shoes on. And he had on some burgundy wingtips with tan ribbed socks! I said to Bono, 'Man, the Pope has got some pimp shoes on. Them Catholics will kill me if they hear that.' If ever I want to crack Bono up, all I've gotta do is say, 'The Pope has some pimp shoes on!'"

As good a laugh as the devilish duo got out of it, the visit also had some seriously good side effects. According to Bono, "Through that meeting, and through the work of the Catholic Church and the Pope, more than 20 million African children are going to school now who would not be going to school." And as Quincy adds, "Because of that trip, we got $27.5 billion debt relief for Mozambique, Bolivia, and the Ivory Coast."

Bono, Q, and Bob Geldof "looking like three foxes eating sauerkraut" after a meeting with Pope John Paul II, which resulted in a $27.5 billion Heavily Indebted Poor Countries (HIPC) debt relief for Mozambique, Bolivia, and the Ivory Coast.

As my "brother go bragh" Bono would wisely say, "You should look at celebritism and success and fame and all that stuff as a currency, and you have to know how to spend it." It should be about helping somebody else, really. ~ Q

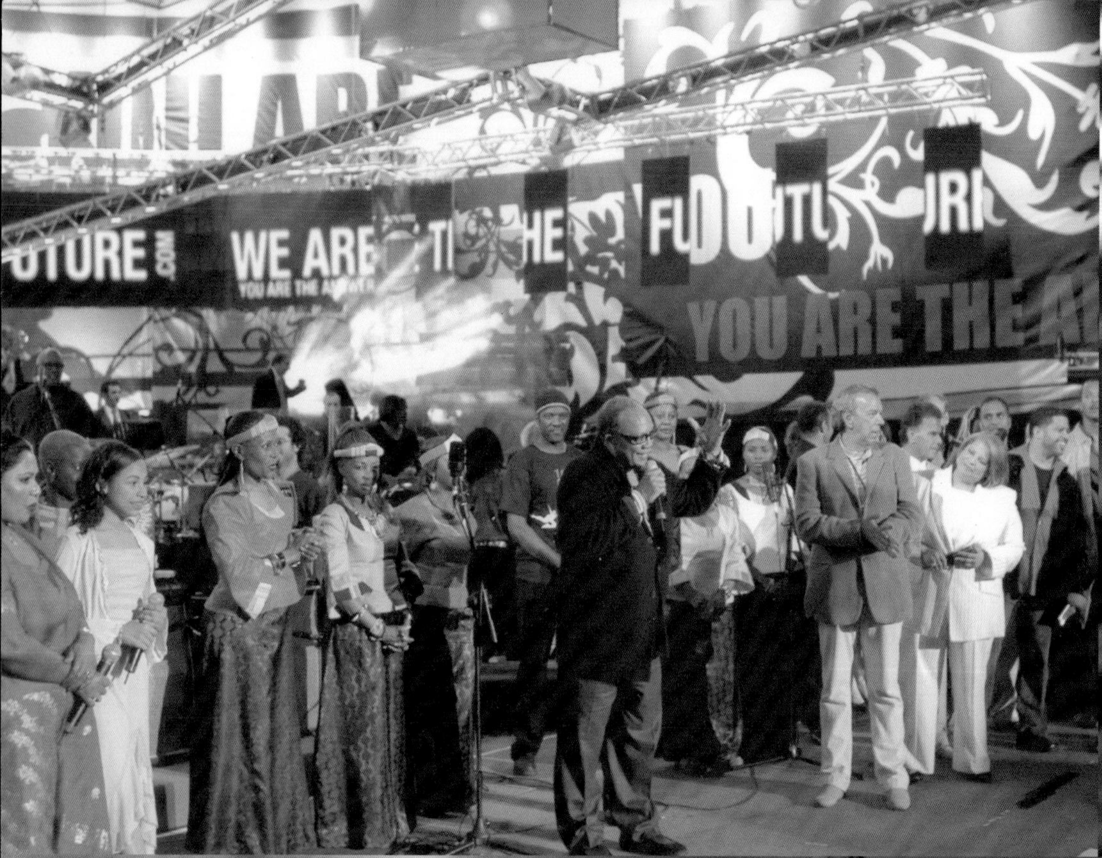
WE ARE
YOU ARE THE
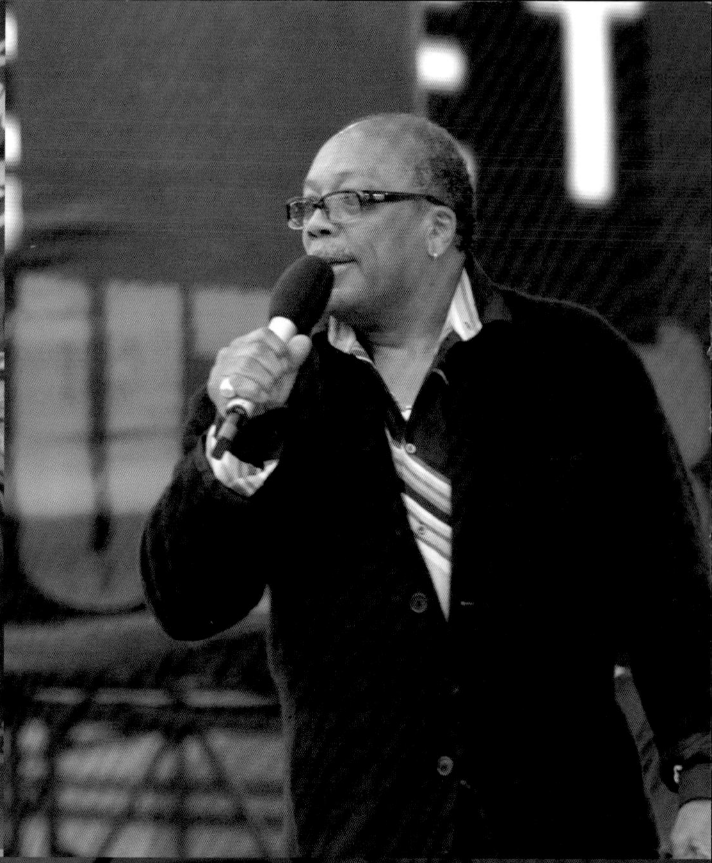
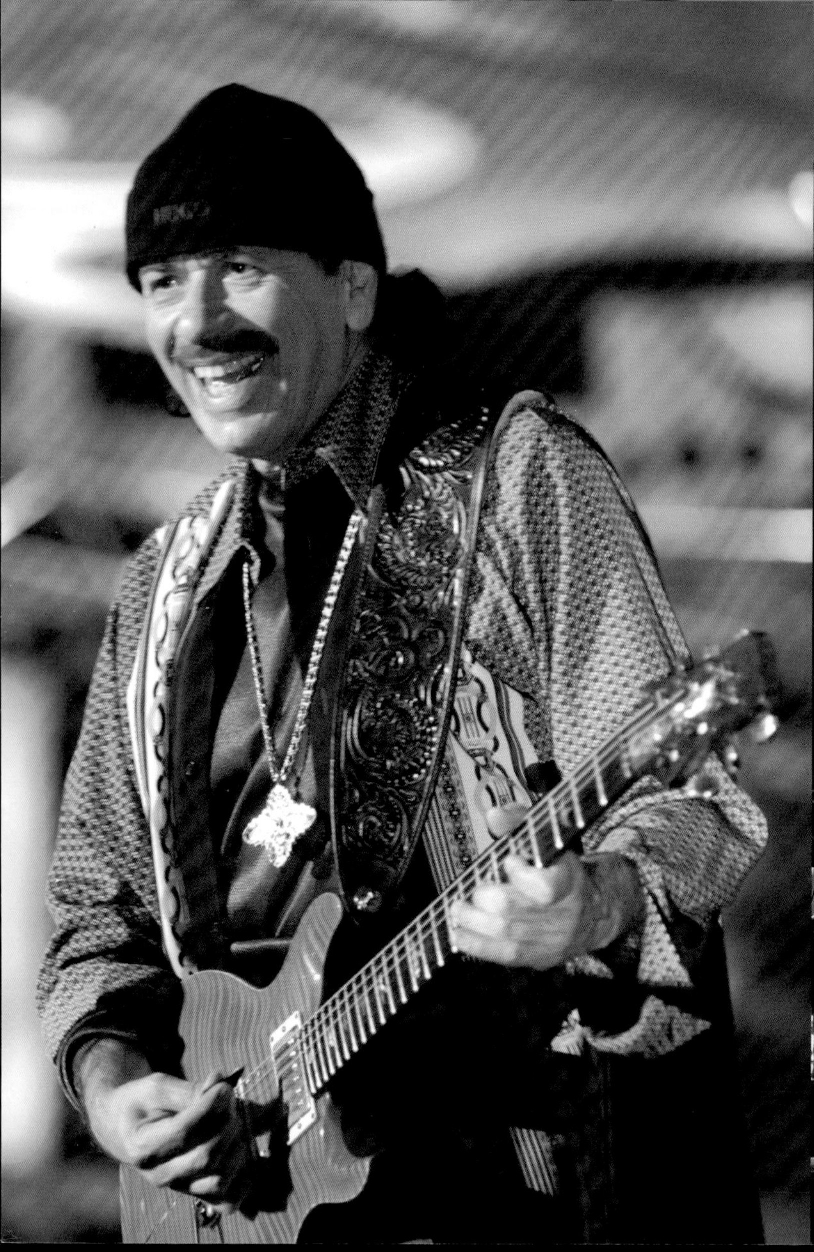
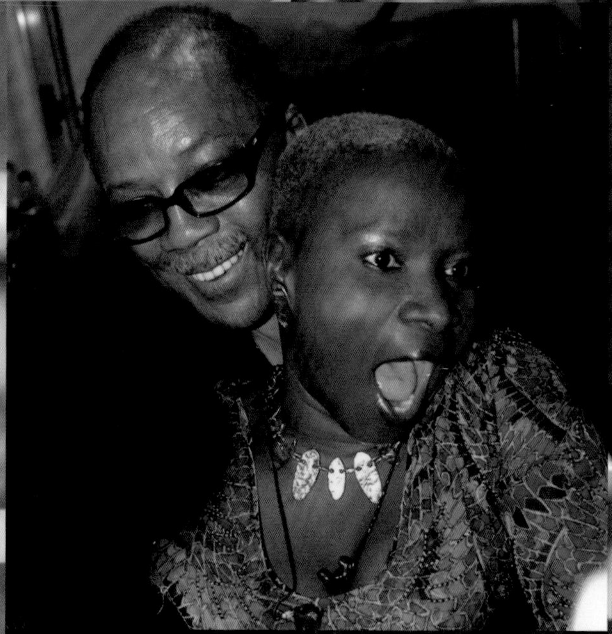
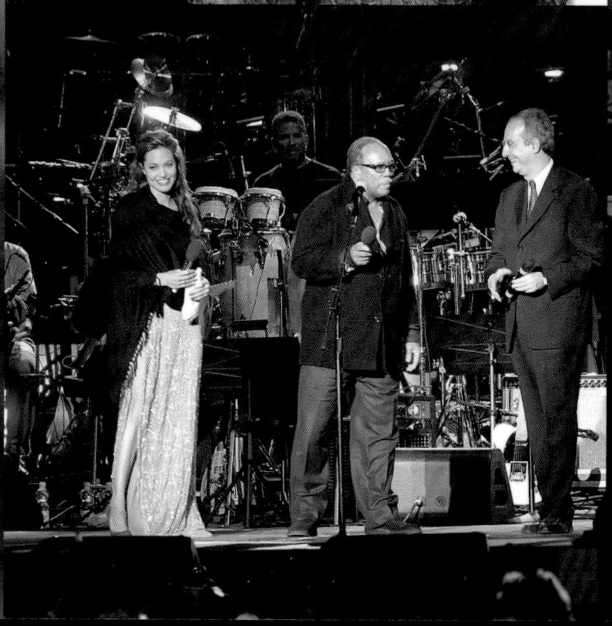
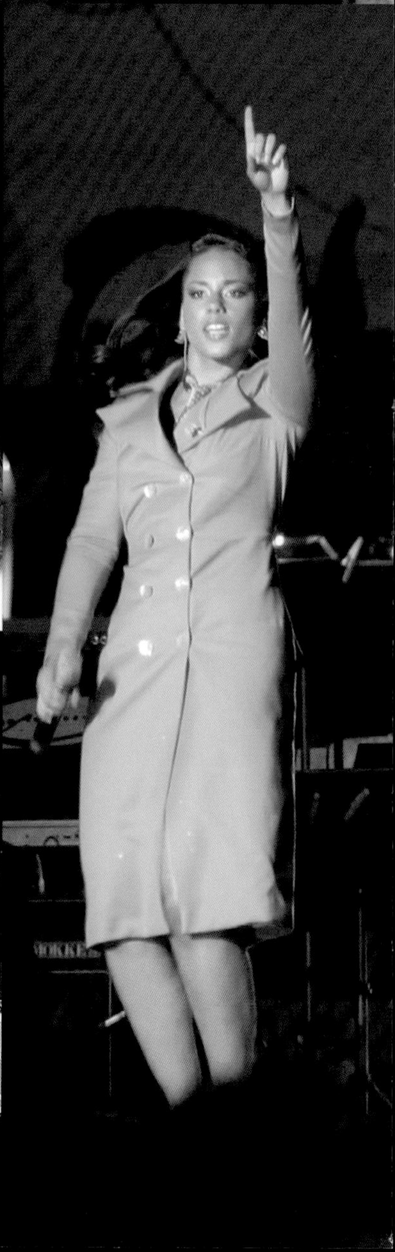

WE ARE THE FUTURE

For all the magnitude of Quincy's twentieth-century achievements, none may prove as far-reaching in impact as the one he'd help get off the ground shortly after the millennium, called We Are the Future. In partnership with an Israeli, Uri Savir of the Glocal Forum, and American-Palestinian businessman Hani Masri (who are best friends), and with support from the World Bank and United Nations, the Quincy Jones Foundation initiated the program in 2004 to improve the lives of children and promote peace in areas of conflict throughout the globe.

We Are the Future launched with a concert extravaaganza graciously hosted by the Mayor of Rome, Walter Veltroni, at Circus Maximus in Rome on May 16 of that same year, featuring the top performers from countries around the world. Fourteen months of preparation went into what Quincy would term a "global gumbo" of music, which included musicians not only from the United States, but also the Europe, the Middle East, South America, and South Africa. Angelina Jolie, Chris Tucker, Evander Hollyfield, Francesco Totti, Naomi Campbell, Oprah Winfrey, Quincy Jones, and Serena Williams, were presenters; Alicia Keys, Andrea Bocelli, Angélique Kidjo, Carlos Santana, Carmen Consoli, Ennio Morricone, Fher (of Maná), Herbie Hancock, Josh Groban, Juanes, Karina Pasian, Kazem Al Sahir, Khaled, Noa, Norah Jones, Patti Austin, Rifat Salamat, Ali Kahn, Simon Shaheen, Soundz of South Afrika, Stomp, and Take 6 performed,

"We all know that the world is a total mess right now, and doing nothing about it is no longer an option, especially when it comes to children," Quincy announced to the half-million-strong crowd. "We Are the Future is dedicated and committed to helping the kids from being deprived of a God-given right to have a family and good health and an education and hope. We all desperately need to build bridges to each other and respect each other's differences. And always remember that love sings louder than hate. That's why children are the future, and you and we are the answer."

Today, just a few years later, We Are the Future's impact has been substantial, with children's centers set up in Addis Ababa, Ethiopia; Asmara, Eritrea; Freetown, Sierra Leone; Kabul, Afghanistan; Kigali, Rwanda; and Nablus, Palestine, the last organized in a peace-building partnership with the city of Rishon LeZion in Israel. The centers have youth-led activities focusing on five areas deemed particularly essential: health, nutrition, arts, sports, and information communications and technology. It might take quite a while for changes to take root in isolation, so each center is linked to the developing world by city-to-city partnerships as well.

Stresses Quincy, "People have to be on the same course; they have to be going the same way. That's what music is about, and that's all I know. 'Cause when you put a rhythm section together, there's a bass player, a drummer, a guitar player, and a piano player. They all do something different, but they do exactly the same thing. And that's what it feels like. It feels like a rhythm section. A world, global universal rhythm section of knowledge, experience, compassion, and understanding. And I love it, I love being a part of it. I really do."

As Quincy declares, "Peace is possible, and children are the answer if we give them the tools to create better lives. Abandon them, and chaos and hate will rule their future. Every child on this planet has a God-given right to a common destiny."

*M*y instrument is playing all these things. Playing the singers, playing the songs, playing the musicians, and seeing that big vision. It's like a huge collective, creative tapestry. ~ Q

top right: With Rod Temperton.

opposite, clockwise from top left: L to R: Riffat Sultana, Karina Pasian, The Soundz of South Afrika Choir directed by Caiphus Semenya, Q, Rod Temperton, Patti Austin, and Take 6

Q addressing the crowd.

Alicia Keys.

Onstage with Angelina Jolie and Walter Veltroni, mayor of Rome.

Carlos Santana.

center: Angélique Kidjo.

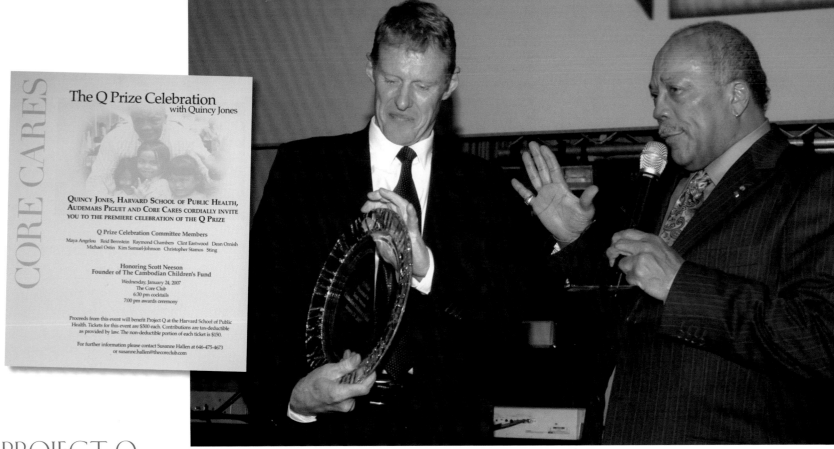

PROJECT Q
WITH HARVARD

QUINCY DID NOT complete his college degree before setting out on his course as a professional musician. But he knows how important colleges are both to educating youth and making some of his programs happen, and he has worked extensively with institutes of higher education to promote musical scholarship and philanthropic endeavors. In the past decade, in fact, he's been both active with and venerated on several occasions by Harvard University, perhaps the most respected such institute in the United States. This association is also in keeping with his fervent wish to leave a humanitarian legacy; Harvard's been around for several hundred years, and will likely be around a good long while.

In 2000, the university established the Quincy Jones Professorship of African-American Music. Created with a $3 million gift from Time Warner Inc.,

it was not only the first endowed professorship in African-American music at Harvard, but possibly the first in the country. Time Warner Chairman and Chief Executive Officer Gerald M. Levin put it this way at the press conference where the endowment was announced: "It honors music, which is a fundamental art form, and it honors Quincy Jones, probably the most unique individual in the history of music."

Chimed in Harvard's African American Studies Department Chair, Henry Louis Gates, Jr., whose *Africana: The Encyclopedia of the African and African American Experience* help fund the endowment, "Music has been central to the African American experience since slavery. And few, if any, cultural developments in the twentieth century have been as important as the creation of jazz. Thus, it is especially fitting that Time Warner should honor both African-American music and

one of its undisputed masters by endowing the Quincy Jones Professorship of African American Music." As Gates later elaborated, "Quincy was smart enough to figure out how the system works and talented enough to master it. He's a role model for a whole new generation of black artists."

His many ties to Harvard include being the commencement co-speaker (with Madeline Albright) in 1997, the recipient of a Harvard Foundation for Intercultural and Race Relations award in 2004 and an honorary doctorate in 2008, and being the proud father of an alumna, Rashida.

Most significantly, Quincy's also worked with the university to launch Project Q, a Harvard School of Public Health initiative to mobilize advocacy, awareness, and resources benefiting children worldwide. He's always been a magnet for the media spotlight, but

Project Q will use that spotlight for a purpose other than bolstering his own profile: instead, it will use the power of the mass media to direct urgent attention to initiatives for helping the kids who are both near to his heart and vital to implement for the planet's future, especially in conflict regions afflicted by malnutrition and infectious diseases. It doesn't stop there; the nature of the mass media itself will be addressed, with journalists from the developing world being brought to Harvard and vice-versa to foster cross-cultural understanding of and exposure to these crucial issues.

Along the same lines, Quincy and the Harvard School of Public Health have devised a new honor, originating the Q Prize to "improve the health and well-being of children worldwide." It's not enough for Quincy to simply mentor; it's also time to use his clout to innovative leadership programs that pro-

vide young people with mentorship, and it's no accident that Project Q was developed by Quincy, Jennifer McCrea, and Jay Winsten, Associate Dean of the School of Public Health. The two became friends when Winsten reached out to the Hollywood community for a youth violence prevention program in the 1990s, Quincy becoming a spokesperson for a Harvard mentoring project geared toward at-risk kids. Winsten was impressed by Quincy's sincerity and dedication, and Quincy—always one to keep up with street culture—was in turn impressed that a Harvard dean knew who rapper Method Man was.

In 2007, the first Q Prize was awarded to Scott Neeson, executive director of the Cambodian Children's Fund, who'd given up a high-paying job to work on behalf of Cambodian youth. Neeson, on a backpacking trip, had seen destitute children scavenging through mountains

of garbage. Project Q's raised more than $600,000 for Neeson's program, generously donated by Tony Robbins, Donna Karan, and Dean Ornish. Yet apart from supplying needed funding, the hope is to use innovators like Neeson as an example of how enormous a good can be done in situations that look hopeless on the surface. The plan for the future is for the Q Prize to recognize not just one individual per year, but to spread the awards among several individuals in different categories annually.

Also in 2007, the Harvard School of Public Health in turn recognized Quincy's humanitarian contributions by honoring him its first ever Mentor of the Year. Jay Winsten summarized it nicely: "Quincy Jones's entire life is a testament to the power of mentoring. He has served as a role model for using the power of celebrity to improve the lot of humankind."

Q receiving Mentor of the Year award from Harvard University, with Usher (L) and Jay Winsten.

opposite: Scott Neeson receiving the first annual Q Prize.

BEIJING OLYMPICS

QUINCY ALSO SHOWs no signs of slowing down in his humanitarian efforts. Asked to serve as a culture and art consultant for the 2008 Beijing Olympics, as the event drew near he met with the Chinese Ambassador to the United Nations, Vice Foreign Minister Wang Guangya; Ambassador Liu Guijin, China's Special Representative on Darfur; and addressed Chinese business and cultural leaders. The topic was not so much art and culture as Quincy trying to open a dialogue for concern over China's human rights record, especially in Sudan's Darfur region, for which China has supplied weapons and economic support to the military. "I don't pretend to be a politician," he told the Associated Press. "I'm just a musician who cares. We're talking about babies dying in Darfur, so that one has got me personally.

"Over the past couple of months, I've received dozens of protest letters from various groups, here and abroad, begging me to boycott the Beijing Olympics. The pressure from all directions has been extremely intense. It's not my intention to withdraw from the Olympics. I care too much about Darfur and China, and if I can stay in the game with others like us, I feel we can make a difference. The whole world has got to start taking responsibility for each other. With communication, you can no longer afford the luxury of thinking of national kinds of issues. Everything that's done anywhere is a world issue, and together there's lot of things we can do that nobody can do alone."

top: With a top government official in the city of Xi'An.

bottom: "It's good to be the emperor—even if you're 2000 years late!"

opposite, clockwise from top left: "I've been friends with Jackie Chan since I produced the Academy Awards in 1996 and he did the Long and Short Subjects award with Kareem Abdul-Jabar. This is at a dinner in Lan Kwai Fong in a restaurant owned by my dear friend Allan Zeman."

Q calls Yue-Sai Kan, China's Oprah, "my brilliant baby sister." This was taken in Shanghai.

With musician playing the guzheng.

Entrance to the city of Xi'An. The mayor laid down the drawbridge and opened the city gates, then granted Q a key to the city. In the background is a crowd of about 100,000 people.

Quincy has always had an enormous amount of empathy, feeling, for other people. He always understood that people needed a way of living that brought them together and made them feel good about themselves inside, that they're really two sides of the same coin, and in the end you can't feel gaood about yourself inside if you're mistreating people who are different from you or oppressing them or looking down on them.

~ PRESIDENT BILL CLINTON

5

LIFE &
LEGACY

You make a living with what you get,
and you make a life with what you give. ~ Q

LIFE & LEGACY

WHEN A MAN DOES as much for as many decades as Quincy has, it's hard in the end to say what's made the most difference to the millions—if not billions—who have been affected by his work. If you go by the raw figures that seem to matter most to our commercial media, those 50 to 100 million copies of *Thriller* would surely stand out; so would the billion or so dollars directly or indirectly raised for African aid by "We Are the World." If you go by the hippest of critics not likely to be impressed by sales tallies or chart statistics, there are all those records he produced by jazz legends and Frank Sinatra, as well as his own discs as a leader of big bands both jazzy and funky. If you're looking at the impact he's had on African-American culture, there are few if any role models who've shown how a black citizen of the United States can rise to the highest levels of power in the record and film business, whether in the studio, on the set, or at the boardroom.

He has more Grammy nominations (79) and has won more Grammys (27) than any other living person. He is the African American with the most Academy Award nominations (tied, at 7), and is the only black film producer to be nominated for "Best Picture." He holds the rank of Commandeur of the Légion d'Honneur, on top of Kennedy Center Honors, the Rudolph Valentino Award (Italy's highest artistic honor), the Polar Music Prize (Sweden's highest artistic honor), and dozens of others.
But what Quincy sees as the greatest legacy he can leave has little to do with any gold disc, award, or profit margin. Asked these days what he sees as his legacy, he unhesitatingly replies, "To give back. I want to be around my kids, my friends more, but basically to give back, to do something that will outlive you."

Receiving his appointment as Officier of the Legion d'Honneur.

previous page: "My family at a photo shoot for our 2007 Christmas card. They mean the world to me."

It hasn't always been as easy to put that credo into practice as it is these days, when Quincy has the time and maturity to help start and run plenty of projects not strictly tied to making music or advancing his own career. Any full-time musician has to spend a lot of time on the road and in the studio, but as Quincy's since admitted, his workaholic habits have kept him from spending as much time with his kids as he would have liked, especially when he was a young man on the make. He's made up for that some by establishing closer contact with his children—now ranging in age from their teens to their mid-fifties—in his later years. And while it's not quite a substitute for being a Dad, he's also done a lot to help plenty of people from all walks of life much younger than himself by mentoring a posse of musicians and actors, as well as getting philanthropic projects off the ground that help to make life better for the youth all over the world most in need of a hand.

"I've been driven all my life by a spirit of adventure and a criminal level of optimism," Quincy's acknowledged. "I believed in my dreams because they were my only option. The people who make it to the top—whether they're musicians or great chefs or corporate honchos—are addicted to their calling." Yet, at the same time, Quincy can't emphasize enough that "you have to honor the gift God has given you. In a way, the rest of my life has been about trying to honor my gift and the gifts of the many extraordinary people I've encountered along the way. So many

left: With Jolie in Paris c. 1957.

top: With Martina.

people have extended the hand of friendship, of shared creativity, of pure and unadulterated love to me in the course of my life. Thank God and these generous souls for making it feel so natural to give back unconditionally."

You also have to be able to receive as well as give, and learn from those younger than yourself as well as teach them the tricks of the trade. Take his own kids, for example, who are foremost in his mind when he confesses, "The only deep regret I have in the entirety of my life is that I didn't know sooner how much I didn't understand about their needs and how to nurture them. They are the best teachers any father could ever dream of having, especially since they are all finding inner peace."

To Quincy, peace isn't just something to establish within yourself, but also an ideal to bring to your relations with other people. He's been a living example of tolerance through the people of different races and backgrounds he's worked and raised families with, and now he wants those feelings to ripple through the world as well. "To me peace

means acknowledging the territory that you're supposed to be in, to respect and grace each other," he explains. "And for people who don't live there, respecting their point of view. It means a lot of things to me, but it starts with respect."

To command that respect, it's likewise crucial to do your utmost to respect the best qualities in both yourselves and others. Spirituality, Quincy believes, is "the greatest testament that any teacher and mentor can have. I think God is inside of each one of us. I've traveled a lot, I know a lot of friends, and I've seen how it works. I think we all have to believe in something and it's a question of just giving the right focus on it, something that's aligned with your heart and your mind and makes you feel like a valuable addition to this planet."

"The older I get, the more I realize how little we have to do with what happens to us. Adolphe Sax was the Belgian who invented the saxophone hundreds of years ago. Ravel uses it in 'Bolero.' Adolphe had no idea that descendents of American slaves would get a hold of that instrument and come

up with Coleman Hawkins, John Coltrane, and Charlie Parker. We think we're in charge of so much, but it's so much bigger than us. But you stay busy, because you're going to get a lot of rest when you're gone."

I f life is an eight-course meal, this time in mine is desert and a fingerbowl. ~ Q

top: With the family for another Christmas card!

right: With Rashida.

1963: Produces #1 hit by Lesley Gore, "It's My Party." Nine more Jones-produced Top Forty singles, including "You Don't Own Me," follow for Gore in the next couple of years. ♩ Wins first Grammy Award for his arrangement of Count Basie's "I Can't Stop Loving You." ♩ Conducts and arranges on Ella Fitzgerald's album *Ella and Basie*. ♩ Publishes and produces Marvin Hamlisch's first composition (co-written with Howard Liebling), "Sunshine, Lollipops, and Rainbows," which becomes a hit single for Lesley Gore.

1964: After arranging "Fly Me To The Moon," he goes on to arrange and conduct Frank Sinatra's second album with Count Basie, *It Might As Well Be Swing*. ♩ Is asked to score Sidney Lumet's *The Pawnbroker*, marking Jones's first such work on a major film. ♩ Pays tribute to his friend and fellow film composer Henry Mancini on *Quincy Jones Explores the Music of Henry Mancini*. ♩ Arranges for Louis Armstrong.

1965: Moves to Hollywood to devote himself to film work, working on mid-'60s scores for *Mirage*, *Walk Don't Run* (Cary Grant's last film), and *The Slender Thread* (Sydney Pollack's first film).

1966: Arranges and conducts Frank Sinatra's live album with the Basie Band, *Sinatra at the Sands*, during a one-month engagement in Las Vegas. ♩ Conducts, composes (with lyricist Jack Lawrence), and arranges "The Pawnbroker" on Tony Bennett's LP *The Movie Song Album*. ♩ Composes theme for and scores TV series *Hey, Landlord*, the first of numerous television scores he'll do over the next decade.

1967: Scores *In the Heat of the Night* and *In Cold Blood*. ♩ Composes theme for and scores TV series *Ironside*. ♩ Music director for *Rodgers and Hart Today* TV special.

1969: Astronaut Buzz Aldrin plays Quincy's arrangement of Frank Sinatra and Count Basie's "Fly Me to the Moon" when landing Apollo 11 on the moon. ♩ Jones's album *Walking in Space* is released, reaching #2 in Billboard's jazz chart and #6 in its R&B listings. ♩ Scores *The Bill Cosby Show* TV series, co-writing theme song, "Hikky Burr," with Cosby himself.

1970: *Gula Matari* reaches #2 in Billboard's jazz chart

and Top Twenty in the R&B listings.

1971: *Smackwater Jack* released, going to #1 in the jazz chart. ♩ Becomes first African American conductor of the Academy Awards.

1972: Helps organize and produce shows for Chicago's Black EXPO with Jesse Jackson along with Cannonball Adderly, Roberta Flack, Jerry Butler, Hermene Hartman, Lena McLin, and Peter Long. ♩ *You've Got It Bad, Girl* released, topping the jazz chart and reaching the R&B Top Twenty. ♩ Composes theme song for TV series *Sanford and Son*. ♩ Produces *Duke…We Love You Madly*, a tribute to Duke Ellington, with Bud Yorkin for CBS television.

1974: Releases highest-charting solo album, *Body Heat*, which peaks at #6 in Billboard's pop chart. ♩ Suffers massive aneurysm in August, undergoing brain surgery only to discover that a second surgery is necessary to prevent a second rupture. ♩ Marries Peggy Lipton.

1975: His Top Twenty album *Mellow Madness* features contributions from the Brothers Johnson; he'll produce and co-compose on four of their double-platinum albums over the next five years.

1955: In March, arranges and conducts Big Maybelle's "Whole Lot of Shakin' Goin' On," which is covered for a huge rock'n'roll hit two years later by Jerry Lee Lewis. ♪ Conducts and arranges on Betty Carter's *Meet Betty Carter and Ray Bryant* album. ♪ Conducts and arranges on Dinah Washington's *For Those in Love* album, the first of half a dozen Washington albums on which he'll work as conductor, arranger, composer, and/or producer. Says Quincy: "I'll always love Dinah for putting her booty on the line by recommending a relatively inexperienced newcomer to work with her in the studio as conductor/arranger/composer and/or producer after hearing the arrangements I did for James Moody. Dinah's the reason I made the transition into the big-time record business. James Moody saved my boody!"

1956: Organized, arranged, and played trumpet with Dizzy Gillespie's band during international goodwill tour sponsored by U.S. State Department through Adam Clayton Powell. ♪ Participates in panel discussion on "The Future of Jazz" at the Newport Jazz Festival. ♪ Arranges on Ray Charles' album *The Great Ray Charles*.

1957: Releases first LP under his own name at the request of A&R head Creed Taylor, *This Is How I Feel About Jazz*. ♪ Becomes musical director, arranger, and

conductor for French record label Barclay Disques. ♪ Studies composition with Nadia Boulanger in Paris. ♪ While at Barclay, produces the first of several albums for Billy Eckstine, *Mr. B. in Paris* with the Bobby Tucker Orchestra. ♪ Marries Jeri Caldwell, with whom he'd had his first child, Jolie. ♪ Write arrangement for first song by Michel Legrand, "La Valse des Lilas."

1958: Meets Frank Sinatra when he and Eddie Barclay are requested to bring a 55-piece orchestra from Paris to back the singer at the Sporting Club in Monaco for a Grace Kelly charity benefit. ♪ Produces *Vaughan and Violins,* which included the very first recording of "Misty," for Sarah Vaughan, also producing many of her subsequent LPs over the next few years.

1959: Assembles and leads orchestra, and orchestrates along with Billy Byers, for Harold Arlen-Johnny Mercer musical *Free and Easy,* which plays in Utrecht, Amsterdam, Brussels, and Paris. Their only album, *The Birth of a Band,* is released the same year.

1960: After *Free and Easy* closes in Paris in February—after only a two-day notice—Jones

tours as leader of the show's big-band orchestra in Europe for the next ten months. ♪ Receives first two Grammy nominations, for Best Arrangement (for Ray Charles' "Let the Good Times Roll") and Best Jazz Performance, Large Group (for *The Great Wide World of Quincy Jones*). ♪ Arranges five of the tracks on Ray Charles' Top Five album *Genius+Soul=Jazz,* including the Top Ten single "One Mint Julep."

1961: Becomes A&R man at Mercury Records, becoming promoted to vice president by 1964, making him the first African American to hold such a position at a major record label, of which there are only six at the time. ♪ Does his first film score, for Swedish film *The Boy in the Tree,* directed by Oscar-winning Arne Sucksdorff. ♪ Conducts, composes, and arranges on Peggy Lee's albums *Blues Cross Country* and *If You Go.*

1962: In August, arranges, conducts, and produces "Soul Bossa Nova" (from his album *Big Band Bossa Nova*), which 35 years later becomes the theme for the *Austin Powers* trilogy.

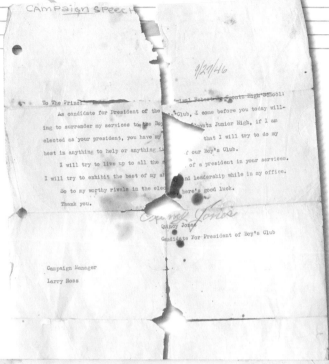

QUINCY JONES TIME LINE

1933: Quincy Delight Jones, Jr., born in Chicago on March 14.

1943: Family moves to Bremerton, Washington, near Seattle.

1945: While in junior high, begins studying trumpet and sings in gospel quartet, and starts to play Seattle clubs.

1947: Moves with family from Bremerton to Seattle, entering James A. Garfield School. ♪ Meets Clark Terry when Count Basie's band passes through Seattle. ♪ Meets Ray Charles, who's recently moved to Seattle, and plays in his band around town.

1949: Is invited to join Lionel Hampton's band and almost does, but is too young to go on the road with him, and resumes his high school education.

1950: Goes to Boston to attend Schillinger House, later known as the Berklee School of Music, on scholarship. ♪ Quincy gets a call to join Lionel Hampton's band. They tour the United States and Canada. ♪ On October 17, makes his first recording as part of Lionel Hampton and His Orchestra, arranging and taking a trumpet solo on "Kingfish."

1951: Oscar Pettiford takes Quincy to New York for a recording session of "Swinging Till the Girls Come Home." Quincy gets to meet many of his idols in person.

1953: Tours Europe and North Africa as member of Lionel Hampton's band, which also includes Clifford Brown and Art Farmer. ♪ Records arrangements in Sweden with Clifford Brown, Art Farmer, and the Swedish All Stars.

1954: Plays in trumpet section on Dizzy Gillespie's *Afro*, the first of several Gillespie recordings on which Jones will play or produce over the next decade. ♪ Arranges album *Helen Merrill with Clifford Brown*. ♪ Conducts and arranges the Treniers' single "Say Hey (The Willie Mays Song)," with guest vocals from none other than Willie Mays himself. ♪ In December, writes and arranges tracks by King Pleasure.

top to bottom: campaign speech, 1946.

Seattle University Band, 1950.

At Shillinger House, 1951.

Quincy Jones NYC 1955

❧ In the summer, organizes symposium of hip-hop performers, diverse leaders, and media figures in New York. ❧ American TV comedy series *MADtv* starts airing in October, co-produced by Quincy Jones Entertainment.

1996: Executive produces the 68th Annual Academy Awards.

1997: Forms Quincy Jones Media Group.

1999: He and partners sell Qwest Broadcasting for a reported $270 million. ❧ *From Q With Love* gives Jones another #1 contemporary jazz album. ❧ Listen Up Foundation sponsors From South Central to South Africa project, and builds 100 homes in South Africa. ❧ As part of the Jubilee 2000 international coalition movement calling for cancellation of third world debt by the year 2000, Quincy, Bono, and Bob Geldof help obtain $27.5 billion in debt relief for Mozambique, Bolivia, and the Ivory Coast. ❧ Executive produces *An American Celebration*, a televised millennium concert, with George Stevens for Bill and Hillary Clinton.

2000: The Quincy Jones-Sammy Nestico Orchestra's *Basie and Beyond* is a Top Ten jazz album. ❧ With a Time Warner grant of $3 million, Harvard University endows the Quincy Jones Professorship of African-American Music.

2001: Publishes autobiography, *Q: The Autobiography of Quincy Jones*. ❧ Box set *Q: The Music of Quincy Jones* is released on Rhino. ❧ Quincy is made a Legion d'Honneur Commander by Jacques Chirac.

2004: With Hani Masri (of Palestine), Uri Savir (of Israel), and Walter Veltroni (the mayor of Rome), Jones launches We Are the Future, an initiative to help children in regions of conflict. Jones produces a concert at the Circus Maximus in Rome in May 16 in front of a live audience of more than 750,000 people to launch the initiative. Travels to Kigali, Rwanda, to open the first of the children's centers after a reception for Paul Kagame in Los Angeles with Oprah Winfrey and Don Cheadle.

2005: Co-produces *Oprah Winfrey Presents "The Color Purple"* on Broadway, which goes on to garner eleven nominations at the 2006 Tony Awards.

2006: The Beijing Organizing Committee for the Games of the XXIX Olympiad appoints Quincy as an Artistic Advisor to the Opening and Closing Ceremonies of the Beijing Olympics.

2007: With Wizzard Media, launches the Quincy Jones Video Podcast, in which he discusses his experiences in the music business. ❧ Composes "I Know I Can," the theme to the 2007 Special Olympics in Shanghai. ❧ Produces "The Good The Bad, and The Ugly" by Herbie Hancock and Celine Dion's "I Knew I Loved You," which is later performed by Dion on the Academy Awards. Championed by Quincy, its composer, Ennio Morricone, is given an honorary lifetime Academy Award.

2008: Announces his first album in nearly 20 years, due out on Qwest/Interscope Records.

left to right: Q.

With Ray Charles.

Hosting *Saturday Night Live.*

Q, Michael Jackson, and Steven Spielberg

Signed poster commemorating his role as producer of the 68th Academy Awards.

We Are the Future concert.

Quincy Jones NYC 1955

❧ In the summer, organizes symposium of hip-hop performers, diverse leaders, and media figures in New York. ❧ American TV comedy series *MADtv* starts airing in October, co-produced by Quincy Jones Entertainment.

1996: Executive produces the 68th Annual Academy Awards.

1997: Forms Quincy Jones Media Group.

1999: He and partners sell Qwest Broadcasting for a reported $270 million. ❧ *From Q With Love* gives Jones another #1 contemporary jazz album. ❧ Listen Up Foundation sponsors From South Central to South Africa project, and builds 100 homes in South Africa. ❧ As part of the Jubilee 2000 international coalition movement calling for cancellation of third world debt by the year 2000, Quincy, Bono, and Bob Geldof help obtain $27.5 billion in debt relief for Mozambique, Bolivia, and the Ivory Coast. ❧ Executive produces *An American Celebration*, a televised millennium concert, with George Stevens for Bill and Hillary Clinton.

2000: The Quincy Jones-Sammy Nestico Orchestra's *Basie and Beyond* is a Top Ten jazz album. ❧ With a Time Warner grant of $3 million, Harvard University endows the Quincy Jones Professorship of African-American Music.

2001: Publishes autobiography, *Q: The Autobiography of Quincy Jones*. ❧ Box set *Q: The Music of Quincy Jones* is released on Rhino. ❧ Quincy is made a Legion d'Honneur Commander by Jacques Chirac.

2004: With Hani Masri (of Palestine), Uri Savir (of Israel), and Walter Veltroni (the mayor of Rome), Jones launches We Are the Future, an initiative to help children in regions of conflict. Jones produces a concert at the Circus Maximus in Rome in May 16 in front of a live audience of more than 750,000 people to launch the initiative. Travels to Kigali, Rwanda, to open the first of the children's centers after a reception for Paul Kagame in Los Angeles with Oprah Winfrey and Don Cheadle.

2005: Co-produces *Oprah Winfrey Presents "The Color Purple"* on Broadway, which goes on to garner eleven nominations at the 2006 Tony Awards.

2006: The Beijing Organizing Committee for the Games of the XXIX Olympiad appoints Quincy as an Artistic Advisor to the Opening and Closing Ceremonies of the Beijing Olympics.

2007: With Wizzard Media, launches the Quincy Jones Video Podcast, in which he discusses his experiences in the music business. ❧ Composes "I Know I Can," the theme to the 2007 Special Olympics in Shanghai. ❧ Produces "The Good The Bad, and The Ugly" by Herbie Hancock and Celine Dion's "I Knew I Loved You," which is later performed by Dion on the Academy Awards. Championed by Quincy, its composer, Ennio Morricone, is given an honorary lifetime Academy Award.

2008: Announces his first album in nearly 20 years, due out on Qwest/Interscope Records.

left to right: Q.

With Ray Charles.

Hosting *Saturday Night Live.*

Q, Michael Jackson, and Steven Spielberg

Signed poster commemorating his role as producer of the 68th Academy Awards.

We Are the Future concert.

1976: The release of *I Heard That*, another #1 jazz and Top-Twenty R&B LP.

1977: Quincy and Gerald Fried's score for first episode of television series *Roots* wins Emmy Award.

1978: *Sounds...and Stuff Like That!* is released, becoming his first solo album to go platinum. ♪ Serves as musical supervisor and scores *The Wiz*, during which he works with cast member Michael Jackson for the first time.

1979: Produces Michael Jackson's *Off the Wall*. ♪ Produces Rufus and Chaka's *Masterjam*.

1980: Starts Qwest Records, whose first album, George Benson's *Give Me the Night*, is released and goes to #4 on the pop chart.

1981: Solo album *The Dude*, the first recording to feature James Ingram's vocals (on "Just Once" and "One Hundred Ways"), goes Top Ten and platinum. ♪ Produces Donna Summer's eponymous album, which includes the hits "Love Is In Control (Finger on the Trigger)" and "The Woman in Me."

1982: Produces Michael Jackson's *Thriller*.

1984: Produces Frank Sinatra's *L.A. Is My Lady*. ♪ Composes the gymnastics theme, "Grace," with Jeremy Lubbock for the 23rd Olympiad in Los Angeles.

1985: On January 28, produces and conducts USA for Africa's "We Are the World" single. ♪ Co-produces, with Kathleen Kennedy and Frank Marshall, Steven Spielberg's film *The Color Purple*, introducing Oprah Winfrey and Whoopi Goldberg.

1986: Suffers emotional breakdown and takes break in Tahiti to recuperate.

1987: Produces Michael Jackson's *Bad*.

1989: His eclectic album *Back On the Block*—featuring contributions from Ella Fitzgerald, Ray Charles, Sarah Vaughan, Miles Davis, Dizzy Gillespie, Herbie Hancock, Chaka Khan, Melle Mel, Kool Mo Dee, Big Daddy Kane, Bono, Steve Wonder, and Ice-T—reaches the pop Top Ten and tops the contemporary jazz and R&B charts. It wins Quincy's first Grammy for Album of the Year.

1990: Forms Quincy Jones Entertainment, of which he is CEO and chairman, in co-venture with Time Warner, Inc. ♪ Guest-hosts *Saturday Night Live*, filmed and broadcast the same night as Nelson Mandela is released from prison in South Africa. ♪ Documentary

Listen Up: The Lives of Quincy Jones released, produced by Courtney Sale-Ross and directed by Ellen Weissbrod. ♪ The hit TV series *The Fresh Prince of Bel-Air*—based on the life of Benny Medina, and produced by Quincy Jones Entertainment, NBC Productions, and Stuffed Dog Entertainment—is launched, introducing Will Smith. ♪ Quincy is made a chevalier of the Legion d'Honneur.

1991: With Courtney Ross, co-founds The Quincy Jones Listen Up Foundation to advocate for youth worldwide. ♪ Produces and conducts *Miles & Quincy Live at Montreux* with Miles Davis.

1993: Executive produces the first official event of the celebration of the inauguration of President Bill Clinton and Vice-President Al Gore, at Lincoln Memorial. ♪ Founds *Vibe* magazine.

1994: In partnership with The Tribune Company, forms Qwest Broadcasting, one of the largest minority-controlled broadcasting companies in the U.S. Appointed to President's Committee on the Arts & Humanities.

1995: At the Academy Awards, is the first African-American to receive the Jean Hersholt Humanitarian Award. ♪ *Q's Jook Joint* released, topping the contemporary jazz chart and reaching the R&B Top Ten.

A BRUSH WITH DEATH

NOTHING MAKES YOU appreciate life more than a brush with death, as Quincy found out in 1974 not once, but twice. Burning the candle at both ends as usual, a searing pain in his head signaled an aneurysm, a congenital weakness in the main artery in the brain roughly equivalent to sixteen strokes, with the main artery delivering blood to the right side of his brain rupturing. "I was in the process of dying then," he feels. "I saw at one point white and gold light. It was sweet; it was blissful, I was so surprised ... except for the pain in my head from the aneurysm."

He defied very long odds by surviving a brain operation, only for the doctors to find a second aneurysm on the other side of his head. "They said the good news is that you lived because there's one out of a hundred that makes it," he recalled in amazement decades later. "The bad news is that you have another one on the other side, and we have to go back in in October. That's when I freaked out. I almost couldn't handle that because I was playing with some crazy odds. Getting in there is no joke. I have two clips on my brain that hold it together so it can never happen again." Unfortunately, he was also instructed never to play trumpet again

to make sure his brain stayed put.

Ever the glass-half-full guy, Quincy feels that good things can come out of bad ones, even near-death experiences. "My aneurysm taught me a lot of lessons," he reflects. "Number one, it taught me how to live. I knew before, but I really learned how to live after that. The doctors that loved me said, 'Say what you feel no matter what it is, get it out, don't hold back nothing, just say what you feel good or bad.'

"When I came out of that hospital, I tell you, the colors of every tree I saw looked totally different. They were more green, the most beautiful green I've ever seen in my life. And looking in people's eyes was like peering into the faces of truth. You just start to deal with things more honestly. It affected me a lot, it made me really appreciate life. I think of what would have happened if I died in 1974, all the things I would have missed if I had not made it in 1974... would have been a drag.

"Three years after my aneurysm, around the time of the formation of Apple Computer, I was astounded to watch the ways and speed with which a computer processes data. Later, in about 1984, Steve Ross insisted I fly up to Atari to meet a guy named Alan Kay—who is our generation's

Einstein and also happens to be a great keyboardist. He's introduced me to some of the smartest people I've met in my life, like Nicholas Negroponte, Ray Kurzweil, and a man named Marvin Minsky and his wife Gloria from MIT—these guys are architects of the future and have been my technological gurus and my homies now for almost thirty years. Marvin Minsky is one of the co-creators of artificial intelligence, and he taught me a ton about the way the mind works and about replicating the human brain.

"Skip forward a few years, and these days I have the distinct pleasure of being taken care of by the best medical minds in the world at the Karolinska Hospital in Sweden. During my first encounter with the head of the hospital, Dr. Tomas Olsson, he enlightened me with the statement that we are all 'self-contained emotional machines.' Between what I learned from Tomas and what I learned from Marvin's book *The Society of Mind,* I had the realization that on that day in 1974 what was going on in my mind during my aneurysm was exactly what happens when a computer dumps data. Dr. Olsson was right."

TAHITI

THOSE WHO LOOK at Quincy's gold records, gallery of awards, and magnificent LA mansion might think he's had a charmed life. The hard cold reality is that those achievements have gone hand-in-hand with several life-threatening crises. He briefly contemplated suicide when his big band was going bust in Europe in 1960; he almost died, twice, when his brain was operated on in 1974. And in 1986—when *Thriller*, "We Are the World," and *The Color Purple* had lifted him to an exalted level of success few entertainers could touch, he found his marriage to Peggy Lipton disintegrating as he teetered close to a nervous breakdown. It was time to cool out. Quincy headed to Papaete, Tahiti, and the nearby islands of Tetiaroa (which his friend Marlon Brando owned), Huahine, Moorea, and Bora Bora in hopes of getting rid of whatever demons were plaguing him.

Bobby Holcomb, a Tahitian artist and musician, introduced Quincy to a fellow artist, a pretty woman named Vaea Sylvain. When she flirted with him, Quincy realized that he wasn't up to it. She told him his Kundalini was gone. That was the moment he realized he really *was* messed up.

Brando had told his staff to put Quincy "on the coconut radio," which is a guarantee that he would have guardians to protect him. "Everyone from the island, artists all, flocked around me. They welcomed me into their lives. They took me on long walks; they fed me what they ate, raw papaya right off the tree served in banyan leaves, raw fish straight out of the ocean served in coconut shells. That was all I ate. I stayed inside alone as much as possible. I did yoga for ninety minutes every day and drank four coconutfuls of water. The Tahitians devoted themselves to making me better. I got used to the jungle life. A whole tunnel opened up in the sky, and it was white and gold, and it went all the way up to heaven ... it was really scary. My soul left my body over there. Phew! It really did, man! I swear to God!"

Natural living is great, but it can't cure everything when you're still on Halcion, a potent medication Quincy was taking to help him sleep that also gave him wicked side effects. Asking a doctor to get him into a sanitarium when he came back to LA, he was instead ordered to get off Halcion pronto, the physician telling his patient "'they used to use Halcion in Korea on prisoners of war for interrogation purposes.' Once I stopped taking it, after two days I started to dream again, literally, and found that my energy came surging back. I felt reborn. I was whole again."

For Q —
We had tears — pain — love and laughter — not enough but we've still got time to 'rock a while.' You taught me much Q, and damn it more I love you. What ever happens we'll always have memories enough for the rest of the season —
Leroy

top: Bobby Holcomb, a famous musician and artist and a member of the "coconut radio" from the island of Huahine in Tahiti, drew this painting, which Q keeps on his bedroom wall. It represents Q's spiritual journey, his learning how to meditate, and the healing process.

bottom: letter from Marlon Brando. Q and Marlon called each other "Leroy" as a private joke.

When life begins to seem like too much, we should take a moment to let the soul catch up with the body. Go out and find a song you love, a poem that touches your heart, and take the time to let the whisper of Heaven's voice come into your mind. Every day that you wake up and are still above the ground—that should be the only reason you need to be happy. ~ Q

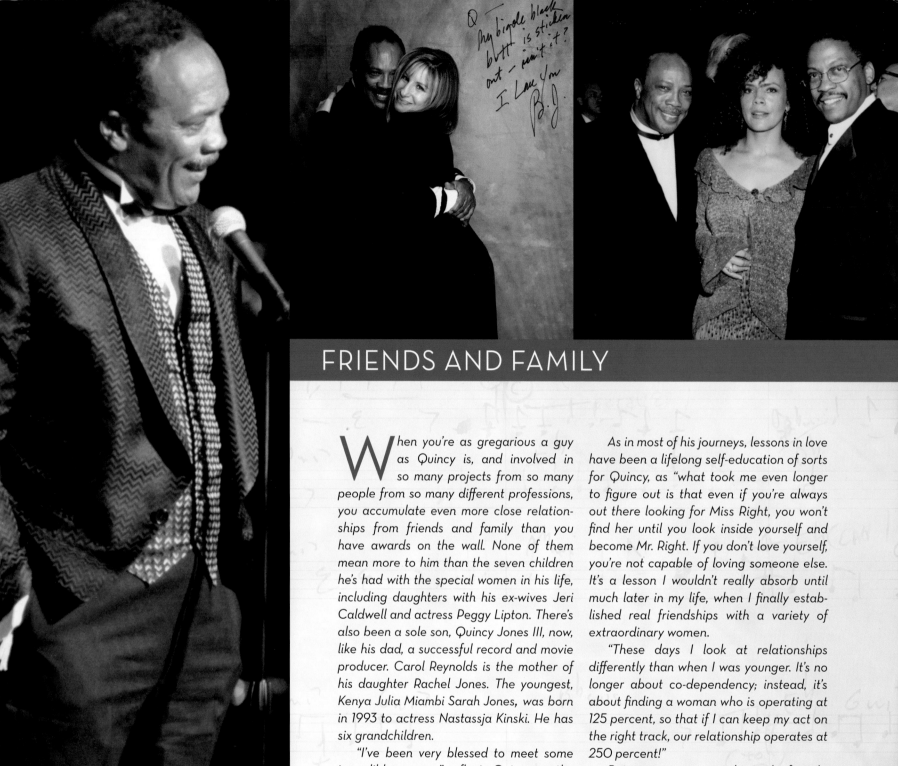

Q — My bignole black butt is sticken out — isn't it? I Love You B.J.

FRIENDS AND FAMILY

When you're as gregarious a guy as Quincy is, and involved in so many projects from so many people from so many different professions, you accumulate even more close relationships from friends and family than you have awards on the wall. None of them mean more to him than the seven children he's had with the special women in his life, including daughters with his ex-wives Jeri Caldwell and actress Peggy Lipton. There's also been a sole son, Quincy Jones III, now, like his dad, a successful record and movie producer. Carol Reynolds is the mother of his daughter Rachel Jones. The youngest, Kenya Julia Miambi Sarah Jones, was born in 1993 to actress Nastassja Kinski. He has six grandchildren.

"I've been very blessed to meet some incredible women," reflects Quincy on the road that's led to such a large brood. "I had my childhood sweetheart Jeri, a fantastic lady. I imagine that the dilemma of my not having a mother had a lot to do with some of the relationships, positive and negative, or not really understanding women. I guess the way God works, he gave me a lot of daughters, and the daughters taught me a lot about the psychology of what women are about."

As in most of his journeys, lessons in love have been a lifelong self-education of sorts for Quincy, as "what took me even longer to figure out is that even if you're always out there looking for Miss Right, you won't find her until you look inside yourself and become Mr. Right. If you don't love yourself, you're not capable of loving someone else. It's a lesson I wouldn't really absorb until much later in my life, when I finally established real friendships with a variety of extraordinary women.

"These days I look at relationships differently than when I was younger. It's no longer about co-dependency; instead, it's about finding a woman who is operating at 125 percent, so that if I can keep my act on the right track, our relationship operates at 250 percent!"

But women are not his only friends. While the world knows the likes of Sidney Poitier, Michael Caine, Oprah Winfrey, Steven Spielberg, Maya Angelou, and Bono only as celebrities, to Quincy they're not just personal friends, but an extended family of sorts. For forty years, in fact, he and Caine have been celebrating their birthdays together after finding out they were born the same year, month, day, and hour, Quincy calling them "celestial twins."

INTERNATIONAL HERALD TRIBUNE, TUESDAY, DECEMBER 5, 1989

Quincy Jones: Black Music's Bernstein

Thriller and Steven was ~~ing E.T. With Spielberg, "It was love at first sight between Steven and me. He had a beguiling way about him, and he was always the same, a very down-to-earth guy by any standard, let alone for a genius." Best friends can be best enemies too, and the pair fell out over a business matter for more than a year soon afterward. But for Quincy, friendship's thicker than blood, and when he bumped into Spielberg on the Aspen ski slopes, "We just stopped and hugged each other. He said, 'I was wrong. We should've never let it get that far.' I said, 'I was wrong, too.' I apologized, and it was over. He likes to say, 'Quincy and I, we've seriously earned our friendship,' and he's right. We got a Purple Heart over it, and God sent down a little gift for both of us the next year in the form of The Color Purple."

Quincy's been there for lots of friends in all walks of life, and inspires the same sort of loyalty in return. Michael Milken, whom Fortune magazine called "The Man Who Changed Medicine" for his 35 years of supporting advances in medical research, is a close companion. His intimates include singers Patti Austin, Siedah Garrett, and, before his tragic death, Marvin Gaye. As Bill Clinton tells it, "Quincy's always got a

smile, doesn't matter how bad ~~ ~ is for me a constant reminder of the power of friendship and heart and spirit."

Record executive Clarence Avant has known Quincy "since before there was electricity." They first met when they were both on the street, that street being the jazz clubs and studios of the late 1950s. He calls Quincy "a dedicated artist, who has the greatest ears of any era, and lives a life like no other man of his, or any other, age. He's a different breed of cat, never sleeps. If he's in town, we hang out a couple of times a week, go catch a jazz act, have dinner. We've traveled together a lot to Europe, Montreux, South Africa. Sometimes we agree to disagree, and I always put ice in my wine at his highfalutin' parties, which drives him nuts. But we can also talk over our problems, and when I say he's a friend, he's a real friend, man."

As Sidney Poitier puts it, "I stand in awe of the man, in a way. I admire him greatly. He has done wonderful things with music and through music. He's left an imprint on the world in which he lived. I have so much admiration and respect for him—that's really what is the foundation of our relationship."

clockwise from top left: Leonard Bernstein giving Q a private tour, discussing Michelangelo's restored masterpieces on the ceiling of the Sistine Chapel.

"If God created a stronger friendship than the bond between Clarence [Avant] and me, he must have kept it for himself."

"With my dear friend and international business guru Michael Milken and Willie Nelson at the Prostate Cancer Foundation New York dinner where I received the Hope Award."

L to R: Dr. Dean Ornish; Ernie Wilson, the Dean of the Annenberg School of Communications at USC; Joe Robert of the JER Companies; Q; and Hani Masri, "one of my partners on We Are the Future and my guru supreme!"

opposite, top center: Barbra Streisand, "my dear ghetto baby lady since the age of 16, who is one of the most talented 'everything' artists on the planet."

top right: Q, Jolie Jones, "and my dear old friend Herbie Hancock ... hangin'!"

To Eights my
great friend,
How can anyone
have someone
better steering you
through life
You'll be my skipper
forever so how
can either one
of us miss
I love you
"Aces"
AKA STEVE

"Steve Ross for me was ultimate visionary, brother, mentor, and unconditional friend. There aren't many people who operate at 50 thousand feet that share information—let alone form an alliance—between a $50 billion company and my black entertainment company. He could see around the corner for days—MTV, the Time-Warner merger, Time Warner Cable, the list goes forever. He was 'Aces,' I was 'Eights,' and he will forever remain deep down in my heart. The caption above was written as an inscription—three days before he passed away—on the above photo of a summer vacation in Maine.

Every creative artist who gets his work out to millions of people needs major help on the taking-care-of-business end. In Quincy's case, he was fortunate enough not only to become tight with one of the top entrepreneurs in mass media, but also to count the man as one of his very closest friends. The late Steve Ross—CEO, president, and chairman of Warner Communications—joined with Quincy and Time Warner to create the multimedia company Quincy Jones Entertainment (QJE), and also helped Quincy with the launch of Vibe magazine. QJE, feels Quincy, "is still the model for other black-owned entertainment businesses who've seriously joined forces with a major media company. My friend and mentor Steve Ross understood what 98 percent of corporate America didn't get—the influence of black culture."

In Quincy's view, "The people who achieve greatness in their chosen fields have a core skill upon which they expand. In Steve's case, it was his astounding ability with figures and his photographic memory. He could juggle an extraordinary number of diverse elements and people at one time and keep it all fluent. And neither he nor Bob Pittman [another key figure in QJE, previously famous for being the guiding force behind the rise of MTV] messed around. The vision was followed up by speed-of-lightning execution. They didn't hesitate or fumble. Steve taught me to try to hold on to 25 or 30 percent of anything you sell, and that the last two points in closing any deal are a deadline and a consequence. He also advised, 'Mean what you say,' 'Make it win-win,' 'Be a bear, be a bull, but never a pig,' and 'Always try to return phone calls.'"

Ross once asked him, "Why do you want to do TV and movies?" and Quincy replied, "Because I know inside that I can do it." Ross said "Prove it." Q took him up on it, and the result was The Color Purple.

What Quincy misses most about Steve Ross, though, isn't his sharp head for business, but his friendship and creativity. "We never did anything in his office," he reflects. "It was always on the seashore, somewhere on a boat, just hanging out where our minds were free, and we seemed to be more creative." At Steve's funeral, "I tried to speak, but there was too much to say about this man; my mouth would not respond."

Steve flew all the way to Cannes, France, to surprise me when I was appointed as MIDEM "Man of the Year" and Officier of the Legion d'Honneur.

MEMORIES

TOP ROW L–R: John H. Johnson; Eddie Barclay, Q, Caroline Barclay; Johnny Mathis, Q, Jane Fonda, Steven Spielberg. ROW 2: Q, Terrence Howard, Morgan Freeman; Deborah & Carlos Santana, Salma Hayek, Q; Jerry Allison, Q reviewing plans for Q's new home; John Sie, Q. ROW 3: Q, Céline Dion; Q, Benny Carter; Q, Marvin Gaye; Alan & Marilyn Bergman, Q, Gloria & Emilio Estefan.

opposite: TOP ROW L–R: Q, Lloyd Jones; QD3, Muhammad Ali, Q. ROW 2: Tevin Campbell; Flip Wilson, QD3, Ulla Anderson, Cannonball Adderley, Q, Tina Jones, Roberta Flack. ROW 3: Quincy Sr., QD3, Quincy Jr.; Gayle King, Q; Q, Gloria Jones in Paris.

TOP ROW L–R: Q, Courtney Ross, Steven Spielberg, Steve Ross, Barbra Streisand; Phil Ramone, Russ Teitelman, Phyllis Lubarsky, Claude Nobs, Arif Mardin; Q, Naomi Campbell. ROW 2: Q, Ray Charles, Michael Caine; Q, Halle Berry; Q, Siedah Garrett. ROW 3: John Singleton, Usher, Jermaine Dupri, Chris Tucker, Bono, Q; Bruce Swedien, Q; Ashford & Simpson, Q, Dawnn Lewis.

opposite: TOP ROW L–R: Q, Evelyn & Mo Ostin; LL Cool J, Q, Lloyd Jones. ROW 2: Michael Jackson, Q, Peggy Lipton; Q, Cab Calloway in Paris. row 3: Joe Pesci, Q; Aretha Franklin, Q.

TOP ROW L–R: Q, Eddie Murphy; Toots Thielemans, Cary Grant, Q; Q, Cicely Tyson, Gregory Peck. ROW 2: Greg Phillinganes, Oscar Peterson, Q; Burt Bacharach, Marlene Dietrich; Terry Semel, Nastassja Kinski, Q. ROW 3: Toni Faye, Sammy Jay, Teresa Frank, Charlotte Crawford, Richard Jones, Lesley Jones; Patti Austin, Q; Martin Scorsese, Q.

OPPOSITE: TOP ROW L–R: Robin Williams, Q, Steven Spielberg; Debbie Allen, Q; Q, James Ingram. ROW 2: Herbie Hancock, Heavy D, Q; George Lucas, Q; Q, Sting. ROW 3: Robert De Niro, Q, Nelson Mandela; Bridgid Coulter, Don Cheadle, Oprah Winfrey, Q, Paul & Jeannette Kagame.

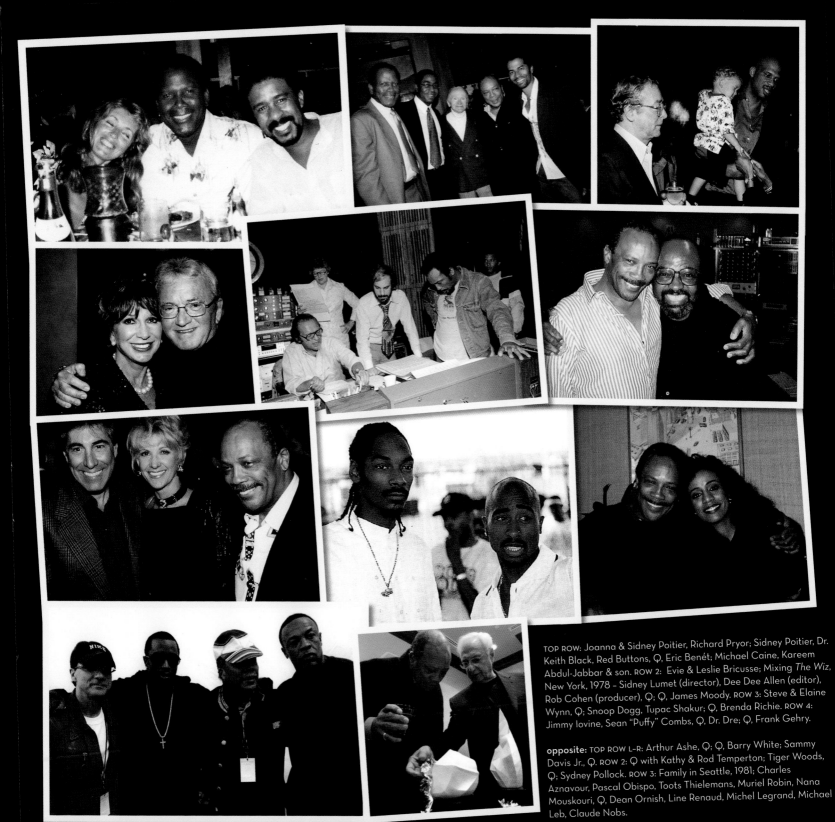

TOP ROW: Joanna & Sidney Poitier, Richard Pryor; Sidney Poitier, Dr. Keith Black, Red Buttons, Q, Eric Benét; Michael Caine, Kareem Abdul-Jabbar & son. ROW 2: Evie & Leslie Bricusse; Mixing *The Wiz*, New York, 1978 – Sidney Lumet (director), Dee Dee Allen (editor), Rob Cohen (producer), Q; Q, James Moody. ROW 3: Steve & Elaine Wynn, Q; Snoop Dogg, Tupac Shakur; Q, Brenda Richie. ROW 4: Jimmy Iovine, Sean "Puffy" Combs, Q, Dr. Dre; Q, Frank Gehry.

opposite: TOP ROW L-R: Arthur Ashe, Q; Q, Barry White; Sammy Davis Jr., Q. ROW 2: Q with Kathy & Rod Temperton; Tiger Woods, Q; Sydney Pollock. ROW 3: Family in Seattle, 1981; Charles Aznavour, Pascal Obispo, Toots Thielemans, Muriel Robin, Nana Mouskouri, Q, Dean Ornish, Line Renaud, Michel Legrand, Michael Leb, Claude Nobs.

TOP ROW L–R: Salem Bin Dasmal, Q, Negin Fattahi-Dasmal; Nicole Richie, Aaliyah, Nina, Kidada Jones, Eliane Henry; Q, Cliff Perlman. ROW 2: Richard Jones, Teresa Frank, Margie Jay, Waymond Miller, Barbara Miller, Janet Jones, Lloyd Jones, Q; Jerry Inzerillo, Denzel Washington, Prudence Solomon-Inzerillo, Paulette Washington; Q, Ottavio "Tai" Missoni. ROW 3: Q, Angela & Margherita Missoni; Letta Mbulu, Caiphus Semenya; Sage & Tony Robbins; Juanes, Louis Moreno, Q, Gabriella Cordero. ROW 4: Q, Sheikh Mohammed El Khereiji; Badr Jafar, Q.

opposite: TOP ROW L–R: Q, Dr. Alan Counter; Q, Phyllis & Dennis Washington; Ray Brown, Q. ROW 2: Q, Jerry Hey; Q, Larry King. ROW 3: John Clayton, Q, Mayor Tom Bradley; Q with Nicole, Clarence, Alex & Jacquie Avant.

I may be the only person on the planet to have attended my own memorial service. In 1974, after my first aneurysm, it didn't look like I'd make it, so my friends planned a memorial service. Well, I made it, but they had the concert anyway. The doctor said, "The good news is you lived through the first one, but you have another, and we have to go back in in two months." He said I could go to the concert, but I couldn't get excited. How do I not get excited looking at Cannonball Adderly, Clifton Davis, Don Cornelius, Marvin Gaye, Billy Eckstine, Paula Kelly, Sidney Poitier, Minnie Riperton, Sarah Vaughan, Joe Williams, Lincoln Kilpatrick, Richard Pryor, Nancy Wilson, Watts Prophets, Airto, Rosalind Cash, Benny Carter, Ray Charles, Gloria Lynne, Roscoe Lee Browne, and The Sylvers? It was at the Shrine, and the neurologist sat with me and Ed Eckstine to make sure I didn't get into trouble. I still have a great picture of Sidney and me hugging each other that night. ~ Q

top to bottom: Receiving the Polar Prize (considered the Nobel of music) of the Royal Swedish Academy of Music from His Majesty King Carl XVI Gustaf in 1994.

The Polar Prize.

His star on the Hollywood Walk of Fame, 1980.

right: The 2001 Kennedy Center Honorees: Van Cliburn, Jack Nicholson, Luciano Pavarotti, Julie Andrews, Q.

opposite top l to r: Platinum record awards for *Back on the Block, Jook Joint, The Dude.*

AWARDS

IF QUINCY JONES had the notion, he could make a whole book out of nothing but lists of the awards he's won over the last half century—a list that bulges to the bursting point if you count all his nominations, too. He was first nominated for a Grammy in 1960, got his first award (of 27 to date) in 1963, and the parade's gone on ever since—not just for Grammys and his Emmy, but all sorts of other recording, television, film, arts, image, and humanities prizes, not to mention at least twenty honorary doctorates from all over the country. Since the early 1970s, there have also been numerous humanitarian awards, and even cross-category honors like his 1995 Jean Hersholt Humanitarian Award at the Academy Awards for bringing credit to the film industry.

They make for an impressive gallery of trophies, whether in a living room or on the printed page. What they really mean to Quincy, though, are reminders of the many benefits his work has conferred onto others, especially the humanitarian prizes that have dominated his awards list in recent years. "As my 'brother go bragh' Bono would say, 'You should look at celebritism and success and fame and all that stuff as a currency, and you have to know how to spend it.' It should be about helping somebody else, really.'"

Giving underprivileged children a better shot at a happy, productive life is one of the causes dearest to his heart, as "every kid on this planet deserves a common destiny, no matter where they come from."

And Quincy continues to learn from those he's helping out, in places he could have never imagined visiting when he himself was fighting to escape the clutches of his disadvantaged neighborhoods in Chicago and Seattle. "I have never seen young people with such character, vision, trust in the future," he told children in Cambodia in a recent visit to that country, where he's traveled as part of a humanitarian trip with UNICEF. He concluded with an Egyptian saying, "*Bewu-zou-doo-kam*, which means: in your presence, the reflection of you on me makes me feel like a better person. Your light gives me life."

Sure, he knows how to work the crowd at celebrity events, and he is now at the point where humanitarian awards are even named after him. But those galas do their share of good, too, with more than $600,000 getting raised for Cambodian children in less than a minute when Quincy presented Scott Neeson with the first Q Prize. "Tolstoy said it the best way I can think of," he made sure to stress at the ceremony. "He said, 'My piece of bread only belongs to me if everybody else has a piece. And nobody has to starve while I eat.' That's something I will never give up as long as I live."

MULTIPLATINUM ALBUMS
Jackson, Michael, *Thriller*, 1982, 27x
Jackson, Michael, *Bad*, 1987, 8x
Jackson, Michael, *Off the Wall*, 1979, 7x
Jackson, Michael, *HIStory:
Past, Present, and Future*, 1995, 7x
USA for Africa, *We Are the World*, 1985, 3x
Campbell, Tevin, *I'm Ready*, 1993, 2x

PLATINUM ALBUMS
Benson, George, *Give Me the Night*, 1980
Brothers Johnson, *Light Up the Night*, 1980
Brothers Johnson, *Look Out for #1*, 1976
Brothers Johnson, *Right On Time*, 1977
Brothers Johnson, *BLAM*, 1978
Campbell, Tevin, *T.E.V.I.N.*, 1991
Jackson, Michael, *Number Ones*, 2003
Jones, Quincy, *Sounds …
and Stuff Like That*, 1978
Jones, Quincy, *The Dude*, 1981
Jones, Quincy, *Back on the Block*, 1989
Jones, Quincy, *Q's Jook Joint*, 1995
Simon, Paul, *There Goes Rhymin' Simon*, 1973
Simon, Paul, *Greatest Hits*, 1978
Simon, Paul, *Negotiations and
Love Songs*, 1988
Streisand, Barbra, *Till I Loved You*, 1988
Young MC, *Stone Cold Rhymin'*, 1989

GOLD ALBUMS
Charles, Ray, *Greatest Hits, Vol. 1*, 1968
Franklin, Aretha, *Very Best Of*, 1998
Ingram, James, *It's Your Night*, 1983
Jones, Quincy, *Walking in Space*, 1969
Jones, Quincy, *Smackwater Jack*, 1971
Jones, Quincy, *Body Heat*, 1974
Jones, Quincy, *Roots*, 1977
Jones, Quincy, *The Wiz* (Soundtrack), 1978
Jones, Quincy, *Boyz n da
Hood* (Soundtrack), 1991
Rufus & Chaka, *Masterjam*, 1979
Simon, Paul, *1964 – 1993*, 1993
Sinatra, Frank / C. Basie/ Q. Jones,
Sinatra at the Sands, 1966
Summer, Donna, *Donna Summer*, 1982

MULTIPLATINUM SINGLES
USA for Africa, *We Are the World*, 1985, 4x

GOLD SINGLES
Jones, Quincy, *I'll Be Good to You*, 1989
Jones, Quincy, *The Secret Garden*, 1990

Receiving the Jean Hersholt Humanitarian in 1995.

AWARDS SHOWN

Row 1 L to R

Special Recognition (the first MTV Video Award ever presented), 1984

Grammy on the Hill Honoree, National Academy of Recording Arts & Sciences, 2007

George & Ira Gershwin Award, University of California Los Angeles, 2007

BBC Jazz Award, Lifetime Achievement, British Broadcasting Corporation, 2006

Daimler/Chrysler Behind the Lens Award, 2006

Distinguished Service Award, Northside Center for Child Development, 1994

American Music Award, Special Recognition, "We Are the World," 1986

Kennedy Center Honoree Medal, 2001

Ted Arison Award, National Foundation for Advancement in the Arts, 2001

NAACP Image Award, Best Jazz Artist, *Body Heat* (one of twelve such)

MusiCares Person of the Year, Special Humanitarian Award, 1996

African Film Award

Frederick D. Patterson Award, United Negro College Fund, 1999

Lifetime Achievement Award, Rose d'Or de Montreux, France, 1991

Raymond & Esther Kabbaz Award, Le Lycée Francais de Los Angeles, 2007

Friends of the Black Emmy Nominees Award of Recognition, 1996 (one of two such)

Gstaad Cinemusic Award, 1997

The HistoryMakers: Entertainment-Maker, 2007

We Are Family Foundation, Mattie J. T. Stepanek Peacemaker Award, 2006

Row 2 L to R

Academy of Motion Picture Arts and Sciences Jean Hersholt Humanitarian Award, 1994

Ivor Novello International Award, British Academy of Composers & Songwriters, 2007

Officier de la Legion d'Honneur, Republic of France, 1990

Presented "in appreciation for his outstanding achievements," on the tenth anniversary of the Walkman's introduction, by Akio Morita, co-founder and chairman of Sony, 1989

Commandeur de la Legion d'Honneur, Republic of France, 2001

Grammy Foundation Board of Directors

Key to the City of Paris, France, 2000

Whitney Young, Jr., Award, National Urban League, "Impresario, Creative Genius, and Humanitarian," 1986

Grammy Living Legend Award, 1990

Grammy, Album of the Year, *Thriller*, 1983

Pied Piper Award, American Society of Composers, Authors & Publishers, 2008

Academy of Television Arts and Sciences, Outstanding Achievement in Music Composition Award, *Roots – Episode I*, 1977

Trumpet Awards Foundation, Lifetime Achievement Award, 2007

Nelson Mandela Award

Spirit of Life, "Man of the Year," City of Hope, 1982

Thurgood Marshall Lifetime Achievement Award, NAACP Legal Defense Fund, 1996

Spirit of Compassion Award, UNICEF, 2005

Row 3 L to R

Grammy, Record of the Year, "We Are The World," 1985

Nesuhi Ertegün Award, MIDEM Conference, Cannes, 1990

Kennedy Center Honoree, 2001

Distinguished Service Award, The Brotherhood Crusade, 1971

Scopus Award, Hebrew University, 1991

Black Radio Exclusive (BRE) Torchbearer's Award, 1996

Republic of Italy's Rudolph Valentino Award, 1995

Heritage Award, Soul Train Music, 1990

W. E. B. du Bois Medal, Dept. of African and African-American Studies, Harvard University, 2000

National Medal of the Humanities, National Endowment of the Humanities, 2000

United Negro College Fund, "The First Fifty Years," 1997

Trumpet "Living Legend" Award, Turner Broadcasting Systems, 1993

SHARE, Inc., Shining Spirit Award, 1998

Luminary Award, "Trailblazer," American Society of Young Musicians, 1988

Lifetime Achievement Award, *Essence* Magazine, 1994

American Black Achievement Award, *Ebony* Magazine (one of four such)

Row 4 L to R

Ebony Music Award, Musician of the Year, Jazz, 1976 (one of four such)

Life Achievement Award, Cairo International Film Festival, 2008

Golden Note Award, American Society of Composers, Authors & Publishers, 1982

Oscar Micheaux Award, Producers Guild of America, 1999

Henry Mancini Lifetime Achievement Award, American Society of Composers, Authors & Publishers, 1999

American Jazz Award, Contemporary Arranger/Composer, 1997

BET Humanitarian Award, 2008

Brazil Songfest Awards, 1968 (one of two such)

Leadership Award, The Grammy Foundation/Starry Night, 2007

Recognition as "Prominent Alumnus, Trustee, and Overseer," Berklee College of Music, 1983

Lifetime Achievement Vanguard Award, National Academy of Songwriters, 1997

Second Chance Humanitarian Award, 2003

Wisdom Award, National Visionary Leadership Project, 2008

ASCAP Wall of Fame, 2004

Grammy Foundation Board of Directors Award, 2007

Amnesty International Lifetime Achievement (Media Spotlight) Award, 1999

BlackBoard Non-Fiction Book of the Year, 2002

Row 5 L to R

Uncommon Height Award, National Council of Negro Women, 2004

Horatio Alger Award, 1995

Crystal Award, World Economic Forum, Davos, Switzerland, 2000

Marian Anderson Award, City of Philadelphia, 2001

Grand Gala du Disque Populaire, 1964

Spirit of Los Angeles Award, City of Los Angeles, 2006

Special Recognition of 20th Anniversary in Music, City of Philadelphia, 1976

WGCI Granville White Lifetime Achievement Award, 1999

Album of the Year: Jazz Fusion, Japan Grand Prix, *Back on the Block*, 1990

NAACP Image Awards, Big Band Album of the Year, *Smackwater Jack*, 1972

Congressional Black Caucus Foundation President's Award

Tribute Honoree, Los Angeles Jazz Society, 2003

Vibe Magazine Fifth Anniversary Founder's Award, 1998

Henry Mancini Institute "Hank" Award, 2001

Diamond Award (inaugural recipient), Recording Industry Association, 1999

Magnum Opus Award for Lifetime Achievement, USC School of Music, 1996

International Association for Jazz Education President's Award, 2002

Candle of Light Award, Morehouse College, 1999

GRAMMY NOMINATIONS AND AWARDS

1960 Best Arrangement: "Let The Good Times Roll" [Ray Charles] (Mercury) • Best Jazz Performance, Large Group: *The Great Wide World of Quincy Jones* (Mercury)

1961 Best Performance By An Orchestra For Dancing: *I Dig Dancers* (Mercury)

1962 Best Performance By An Orchestra For Dancing: *Big Band Bossa Nova* (Mercury) • Best Instrumental Arrangement: *Quintessence* (Impulse) • Best Original Jazz Composition: *Quintessence* (Impulse)

1963 Best Instrumental Arrangement: "I Can't Stop Loving You" [Count Basie] (Reprise) • Best Instrumental Jazz Performance, Large Group: *Quincy Jones Plays The Hip Hits* (Mercury) • Best Performance By An Orchestra, For Dancing: *Quincy Jones Plays The Hip Hits* (Mercury)

1964 Best Instrumental Arrangement: "Golden Boy" - String Version (Mercury) • Best Instrumental Performance, Non-Jazz: "Golden Boy" - String Version (Mercury) • Best Instrumental Jazz Performance, Large Group or Soloist w/Large Group *Quincy Jones Explores The Music Of Henry Mancini* (Mercury) • Best Original Jazz Composition: "The Witching Hour"; track from *Golden Boy* (Mercury)

1967 Best Original Score Written For A Motion Picture Or Television Show: *In The Heat Of The Night* (United Artists)

1969 Best Instrumental Jazz Performance, Large Group Or Soloist With Large Group: "Walking In Space" (A&M) • Best Original Score For A Motion Picture Or Television Show: *MacKenna's Gold* (RCA) • Best Instrumental Theme: *MacKenna's Gold - Main Title* (RCA) • Best Original Score For A Motion Picture Or A Television Show: *The Lost Man* (Universal) • Best Instrumental Arrangement: *Walking In Space* (A&M)

1970 Best Instrumental Arrangement: *Gula Matari* (A&M) • Best Instrumental Composition: *Gula Matari* (A&M) • Best Jazz Performance, Large Group Or Soloist W/ Large Group: *Gula Matari* (A&M) • Best Contemporary Instrumental Performance: "Soul Flower"; track from *They Call Me Mr. Tibbs* soundtrack (United Artists)

1971 Best Pop Instrumental Performance: *Smackwater Jack* [album] (A&M)

1972 Best Original Score Written For A Motion Picture: *$ Soundtrack* (Reprise) • Best Instrumental Arrangement: "Money Runner"; track from *$ Soundtrack* (Reprise) • Best Pop Instrumental By Arranger, Composer, Orchestra: "Money Runner"; track from *$ Soundtrack* (Reprise)

1973 Best Instrumental Arrangement: "Summer In The City" (A&M) • Best Pop Instrumental Performance: *You've Got It Bad Girl* (A&M)

1974 Best Pop Instrumental Performance: "Along Came Betty"; track from *Body Heat* (A&M) • Best Pop Vocal Performance By A Duo Or Group Or Chorus: *Body Heat* (A&M)

1976 Best Instrumental Composition: "Midnight Soul Patrol"; single from *I Heard That* (A&M)

1977 Best Arrangement For Voices: "Oh Lord, Come By Here"; track from the *Roots* soundtrack (A&M) • Best Inspirational Performance: "Oh Lord, Come By Here" [James Cleveland]; track from the *Roots* Soundtrack (A&M) • Best Instrumental Composition: "Roots Medley (Motherland, "Roots" Mural Theme)" (A&M)

1978 Best Instrumental Arrangement: "Main Title" Overture Part One; track from *The Wiz Original Soundtrack* - Quincy Jones [co-winner: Robert Freedman] (MCA) • Best Instrumental Composition: "End Of The Yellow Brick Road" [Nick Ashford & Valerie Simpson]; single from *The Wiz* (A&M) • Best Arrangement For Voices: "Stuff Like That"; single from *Sounds...And Stuff Like That* (A&M) • Producer Of The Year (non-classical): Best Producer of 1978 - Quincy Jones

1979 Best Disco Recording: "Don't Stop 'Til You Get Enough" [Michael Jackson]; track from *Off The Wall* (Epic) [co-nominee: Michael Jackson] • Producer Of The Year (non-classical): Best Producer of 1979 - Quincy Jones

1980 Best Instrumental Arrangement: "Dinorah, Dinorah" (George Benson) [co-winner: Jerry Hey] (Warner Bros.) • Producer Of The Year (non-classical): Best Producer of 1980 - Quincy Jones

1981 Best R&B Performance by Duo Or Group With Vocal: "The Dude" - Quincy Jones (A&M) • Best Cast Show Album: *Lena Horne: The Lady And Her Music - Live On Broadway* - Quincy Jones, producer [various composers and lyricists] (Qwest/Warner Bros.) • Best Arrangement On An Instrumental Recording: "Velas" (A&M) Track from *The Dude* - Quincy Jones, arranger [Johnny Mandel, synthesizer & string arranger] • Best Instrumental Arrangement Accompanying Vocal: "Ai No Corrida" (A&M) Track from *The Dude* [co-winner: Jerry Hey, instrument arranger] • Producer Of The Year (non-classical): Best Producer of 1981 Quincy Jones • Album Of The Year: *The Dude* (A&M) • Best Pop Instrumental Performance: "Velas"; track from *The Dude* (A&M)

1982 Producer Of The Year (non-classical): Best Producer of 1982 - Quincy Jones

1983 Record Of The Year: "Beat It" (Michael Jackson) (Epic/CBS) - Producer Quincy Jones [co-winner: Michael Jackson] • Album Of The Year: *Thriller* (Michael Jackson) (Epic/CBS) - Producer Quincy Jones, [co-winner: Michael Jackson] • Best Recording For Children: *E.T. The Extra Terrestrial* album (MCA) Producer, Quincy Jones [co-winner: Michael Jackson, Narrator/Vocals] • Producer Of The Year (non-classical): Best Producer of 1983 - Quincy Jones [co-winner - Michael Jackson] • Best R&B Instrumental Performance: "Billie Jean" – (Instrumental version) [Michael Jackson]; track from *Thriller* (Epic) • Best New Rhythm & Blues Song: "P.Y.T. (Pretty Young Thing)" [Michael Jackson]; track from *Thriller* (Epic)

1984 Best Arrangement Of An Instrumental: "Grace" (Gymnastics Theme) - Quincy Jones [co-winner: Jerry Lubbock] *The Official Music Of The 23rd Olympiad In Los Angeles* (Columbia) • Best Rhythm & Blues Song: "Yah Mo B There" [James Ingram & Michael McDonald]; single from *It's Your Night* (Qwest/Warner Bros.)

1985 Album Of The Year: *We Are The World (USA For Africa/The Album)* [various artists] (Columbia) • Record Of The Year: "We Are The World" - USA For Africa (Columbia/CBS) • Best Pop Performance By A Duo Or Group With Vocal: "We Are The World" – single USA For Africa (Columbia/CBS) • Best Music Video, Short Form: "We Are The World" - The Video Event USA For Africa [co-winner: Tom Trbovich, video director]

1987 Album Of The Year: *Bad* [Michael Jackson] (Epic) • Producer Of The Year (non-classical): Best Producer of 1987 - Quincy Jones [co-nominee: Michael Jackson]

1988 Record Of The Year: "Man In The Mirror" [Michael Jackson]; single from *Bad* (Epic) • Trustee's Award

1990 Album Of The Year: *Back On The Block* (Qwest) Producer, Quincy Jones • Best Rap Performance By A Duo Or A Group: "Back On The Block" from *Back On The Block* (Qwest) [co-winners: Ice-T, Melle Mel, Big Daddy Kane, Kool Moe Dee, Quincy D. III] • Best Jazz Fusion Performance: "Birdland" from *Back On The Block* • Best Arrangement On An Instrumental: "Birdland" from *Back On The Block* • Best Pop Instrumental Performance: "Setembro (Brazilian Wedding Song)" [Quincy Jones & various artists]; track from *Back On The Block* (Qwest/Warner Bros.) • Best Instrumental Arrangement Accompanying Vocal(s): "The Places You Find Love" from *Back On The Block* • Producer Of The Year (non-classical): Best Producer 1990 - Quincy Jones • Living Legend Award

1993 Best Music Video, Long Form: *Miles And Quincy Live At Montreux* [Miles Davis & Quincy Jones] (Reprise) • Best Large Jazz Ensemble Performance: *Miles And Quincy Live At Montreux* (Warner Bros.)

1996 Best Instrumental Arrangement With Accompanying Vocal(s): "Do Nothin' Till You Hear From Me" [Phil Collins]; track from *Q's Jook Joint* (Qwest/Warner Bros.) • MusiCares Person Of The Year.

2001 Best Spoken Word Album: *Q: The Autobiography of Quincy Jones* • Best Instrumental Arrangement: "Soul Bossa Nova" [Quincy Jones & George S. Clinton]; track from *Austin Powers International Man of Mystery* and *The Spy Who Shagged Me* scores

2007 Fiftieth Anniversary Ambassador • Leadership Award • Grammy on the Hill Honoree

presents this certificate to

Quincy Jones

On the Grammy Nominated Recording

"Bad"
(Michael Jackson)

in

Album Of The Year

for the awards year 1987

Quincy Jones holds the record for the most Grammy nominations ever, and has more Grammy Awards than any other living artist. **Wins are shown in bold.**

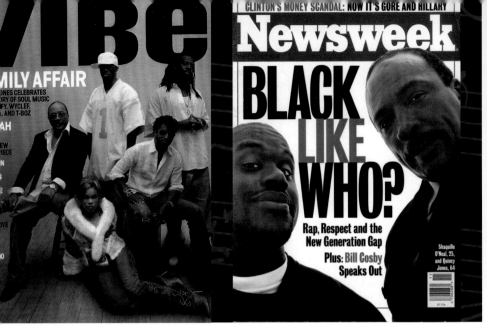

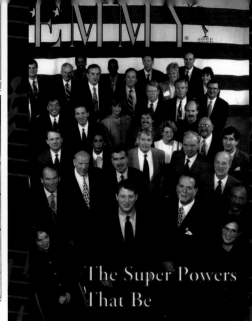

WHAT'S NEXT

ASK QUINCY JONES what he's most proud of and what he most wants to be remembered for, and you might expect him to rattle off a laundry list of accomplishments that would be the envy of almost anyone. Yet so wide is the scope of those achievements, and so long does his to-do list remain, that he frankly responds, "I don't know about that, man. I feel like I'm just starting. Nowadays it's all about my kids. I really love them from deep, deep down. I'm really proud of them, they're all doing such fantastic things."

In the eyes of many, Quincy's reached a stage of his life where he should be slowing down, taking it easy, and wallowing in the glow of his accomplishments. He's having none of it, continuing to push himself with a schedule that leaves little time for idleness, following a drive that's consumed him since he was a child figuring out the lay of the land in his rough Chicago neighborhood. "Since being a little kid I've always believed in taking any negative and finding a way to convert it into something that's positive that's going to work," is his take. "I have a sign on my refrigerator that says, 'God put us on the earth for a special purpose, and right now I'm so far behind schedule I could never die.' But don't get me wrong I can play as hard as I work! And I always feel better saying 'I'm sorry I did' rather than 'I wish I had.'"

Even today, at 75, his energy and commitment is astonishing. At any given moment, Quincy is involved in literally hundreds of projects. At this writing, he is currently in preproduction on eight films, including *Carnaval 3D*, and working on six endorsement deals, a restaurant club in Las Vegas, a Broadway touring show, a stage show, the Olympics, his humanitarian and charity work, *The Complete Quincy Jones*, and an upcoming album being released by Interscope Records, featuring, among others, Snoop Dogg, Jamie Foxx, Akon, Wyclef, Lenny Kravitz, Pharrell Williams, and John Legend.

For Quincy, there's no end to the road of bettering yourself and the lives of others. "You keep figuring it out, you never get it all, but you just have to try," he urges. "I have an affirmation I say every day to myself, that we all can say, that I have conscience divine intelligence, I have direct knowledge of truth, I individualize omniscience, I have perfect intuition and strong spiritual perception, I know and I am because God is guiding me with a divine will to help me to continually build a character that I can love, that I can respect, that I can believe in, that I can live with, so I can better be there for my friends, my family, all my loved ones, and the things I believe in."

Vibe magazine, which Q founded in 1993.

Newsweek, March 19, 1997.

USA Today, June 22, 1999.

Emmy, the magazine of the Academy of Television Arts & Sciences, April, 1994.

Dear G

I Love you because you are you. A world without you would be incomplete. A world with only one you is worth the effort. But a world with one Hundred G,s would Truly be Nirvana.

Thank you for your ThoughtFulness on my Birthday. And Continue to be The Priceless Presence you are in This Troubled world.

Love + Stuff.

Sidney P.

Afterword
SIDNEY POITIER

I REMEMBER FIRST meeting Quincy in the late '50s, when he was appearing at Birdland. I was walking south on Broadway, and he was crossing the street against the light. Several women, on both sides of the street, were ogling him. I knew it had to be Quincy Jones— he was dressed impeccably, and was the most handsome thing you ever saw. We began to talk, and the women just began accumulating. To make his escape, he had to take off suddenly, but left smiles on all their faces.

When my acting career took off a few years later, I knew about his arranging and composing, and studying in Paris, and very much wanted him to score my films. I passed along my great confidence in him to those who were producing and directing, and he was hired for *The Slender Thread*, and, two years later, for *In the Heat of the Night*. We worked together this way on six films, all told.

Friendships come in tones and textures that are indescribable. When personalities like ours come together, it results in a very lasting experience. Our families have become very close, as well. He is what he is; I've never seen him change. The man I met crossing the street against the light—that's a great metaphor of how he lives his life—is the man I know today.

There's not nearly enough paper in the world to address all the good he's done. He is a man of his times, and the times of his life were clam-jammed with admirable intentions, most of which were realized. Quincy is a giving person, an immediate person, and is well informed and well advised on so many issues. He has a huge heart, and incessantly gives of himself, his wherewithal, his material resources, and his time in communal ways to the world around him, and it is a richer place for it.

ACKNOWLEDGEMENTS

WRITING ACKNOWLEDGEMENTS for a book of this sort is so difficult because the truth is I want to thank everyone who's ever been a part of my life and I want all my friends and family to feel appreciated.

First, there are some specific people who helped pull this book together that I need to thank: my best friends Maya Angelou, Clint Eastwood, Bono, Sidney Poitier, and Clarence Avant for sharing in this incredible project with me and, most of all, for being a part of my life and making it such an enjoyable journey. Gloria "GG" Jones, my sweetheart of a sister-in-law, who has managed my archive for the last several years—it was your care for me in every way that resulted in this amazing book. I'd also like to especially thank my late brother Lloyd, who collected many of the assets that were used to create this book. Lloyd, I think about you every day and love you from the bottom of my heart. Another huge shout out to my late brother Waymond, whom I also love and miss every day.

To my dear and cherished "Chewish" little brother, Adam Fell, who has a future so bright it singes my eyebrows: more and more I don't have to finish my sentences; you've got that "can't dance" business mentality! The biggest thank you I could ever give to Debborah Foreman for keeping my life on track—I swear I couldn't do it without you and your incredible team—Shaun Lee and Fabiola Martinez. Debborah, I'm still waiting for my "stepping" pictures!

To my treasured and incomparable publicist, Arnold Robinson, who has kept me in and out of trouble for the last fifteen years! Big thanks to my financial team: Stephen "Sprough" Prough, John "Lamb Chop" Cannon, and Kathy Cannon. To Kimiko Fox, who I'm absolutely thrilled to say is "Back on the Block!" To my "magic-in-the-kitchen" makers—las mujeres mas simpaticas, intellegentes, y bonitas en todo el mundo—lo digo con todo mi corazon; mis hermanitas: Maria Bonilla, Martha Garcia, Ana Jaco (who's been with me since before two of my daughters!), Sandra Coria, and Irene Turner—my second family who all help make my home a home. Also Glenn Fuentes (the best road dawg in the world!) and Joe "Stash" Rivera and their incredible team that keep me safe: Efrain "Nightwatch" Vazquez and Michael "Fo-Oh-Fy" Davis.

To everyone at my music publishing company—Nancie Stern, Joel Sill, Marc Cazorla, and everyone at Cherry Lane. To the QJP interns and employees who helped on this book: Rebecca Sahim, Marston Hefner, and Elizabeth Paich. To Constance Schwartz, Adam Shulman, Kai Henry, Anthoni Allen, and all my friends at The Firm. To everyone who works with my foundations—Jennifer McCrea, Chris Stamos, Jay Winsten, Susan Moses, John and Anna Sie, Chip Lyons, Colin Powell, Madelyn Bonnot, Anders Bjorkland, Ray Chambers, Paul Kagame and his team, Kevin McGovern, Joe Roberts, Kim Samuel-Johnson, Dean Ornish, Tony Robbins, Donna Karan, Salem and Negin-Fattahi Bin Dasmal, Mohammed El-Khereiji, Badr Jafr, Mohammed Jameel, John Woldenberg, Adam Sender, Jeff Walker, Dan Osheyack, Amy Nauiokas, Wes Edens, and Orin Smith. To all of my doctors, including Richard Gold, Joe Sugarman, Larry Norton, Luigi Grattom, Keith Black, Tomas Olsson, Alan Counter, and everyone at the Karolinska Institutet. To my treasured attorney Don Passman and his team—Chuck, Gregg, Gene, and Helen. Thank you to Palace Press for working tirelessly on this book—Raoul Goff, Michael Collopy, Barbara Genetin, Mark Burstein, Michael Madden, Peter Beren, Richie Unterberger, Lucy Kee, Elzer Ramos, Kym Coffey and the rest of the incredible staff. The people who brought this opportunity my way: Robert Thorne, Greg Redlitz, Adam Cunningham, Craig Rosen, Eric Stein, Andrea Brent, Ross Misher, Erik Hyman, and everyone at Loeb & Loeb.

I'd also like to thank all of my mentors, friends, and heroes that were there for me along the way as well as the hundreds of friends that I've lost in the last couple years. A special salute to the bandmates I started out with who are no longer here, including Tommy Adams, Billy Johnson, Charlie Taylor, Major Pigford, Oscar Holden, Grace Holden, Eddie Beard, Harold Redmond, and Bumps Blackwell.

Thank you to all of my wonderful, treasured godchildren. To all the magnificent survivors of the "holocaust of 410," my brother and sisters—I love you all so much. It is my entire extended family to whom I owe the most—and my children and grandchildren who are my inspiration to do everything I do. Jolie, Tina, QDIII, Rachel, Kidada, Rashida, Kenya, Donavan, Sunny, Eric, Jessica, Renzo, Linnea, Koa, Tony, and Mary—words can't describe how proud of you I am. Follow your dreams and never forget that I love you to bits and couldn't do a book like this without all of you. When it rains, get wet, yawl! I am more than blessed to have you all in my life.

PHOTO CREDITS

COLOPHON

Publisher & Creative Director: Raoul Goff
Acquisition Editors: Peter Beren & Michael Madden
Art Director: Iain R. Morris
Designer: Barbara Genetin
Design Assistants: Gabe Ely & Christopher Maas
Design Coordinator: Donna Lee
Managing Editor: Jake Gerli
Project Editor: Mark Burstein
Project Writer: Richie Unterberger
Editorial Assistant: Lucy Kee
Project Liaison to Mr. Jones: Michael Collopy
Production Management: Lina S. Palma-Temena & Leslie Cohen
Production Assistant: Hans Hunt

Insight Editions would also like to thank Ethan Boehme, Adam Fell,
Ben Fong-Torres, Sandra Hay, Gloria Jones, Elzer Ramos, Rebecca Sahim,
Robbie Schmidt, Eric Stein, Robert Thorne, and Melanie Wicker.